A Functional Approach to Syntax

In Generative Description of Language

Mathematical Linguistics AND Automatic Language Processing

•

A GROUP OF MONOGRAPHS *and* TEXTBOOKS

•

GENERAL EDITOR:
David G. Hays
State University of New York at Buffalo

1

DAVID G. HAYS (ED.)
Readings in Automatic Language Processing, 1966

2

DAVID G. HAYS
Introduction to Computational Linguistics, 1967

3

FERENC KIEFER
Mathematical Linguistics in Eastern Europe, 1968

4

HENRY KUČERA *and* GEORGE K. MONROE
A Comparative Quantitative Phonology of Russian, Czech, and German, 1968

5

ROBERT R. FREEMAN, ALFRED PIETRZYK, *and* A. HOOD ROBERTS (EDS.)
Information in the Language Sciences: Proceedings of the Conference held at Airlie House, Warrenton, Virginia, March 4–6, 1966, under the Sponsorship of the Center for Applied Linguistics, 1968

6

LUBOMIR DOLEŽEL *and* RICHARD W. BAILEY (EDS.)
Statistics and Style, 1969

7

PETR SGALL, LADISLAV NEBESKÝ, ALLA GORALČÍKOVÁ, *and* EVA HAJIČOVÁ
A Functional Approach to Syntax in Generative Description of Language, 1969

PETR SGALL

LADISLAV NEBESKÝ

ALLA GORALČÍKOVÁ

EVA HAJIČOVÁ

Charles University, Prague

A Functional Approach to Syntax

In Generative Description of Language

AMERICAN ELSEVIER PUBLISHING COMPANY, INC.

NEW YORK - 1969

AMERICAN ELSEVIER PUBLISHING COMPANY, INC.
52 Vanderbilt Avenue, New York, N.Y. 10007

ELSEVIER PUBLISHING COMPANY, LTD.
Barking, Essex, England

ELSEVIER PUBLISHING COMPANY
335 Jan Van Galenstraat, P.O. Box 211
Amsterdam, The Netherlands

Standard Book Number 444-00045-3

Library of Congress Card Number 69-11152

Manufactured in the United States of America

Preface

The present book sums up a certain stage in the research on algebraic linguistics being pursued at Charles University, Prague. It is based mainly on P. Sgall's book (1967a, in Czech), which represents the first attempt at a systematic formulation of the conception of generative description that has gradually been elaborated by our research group. Thanks to the collaboration of L. Nebeský and A. Goralčíková, the present English version also contains a mathematical formulation of the formal properties of the proposed type of description. The English translation, as well as many improvements made with a view to the English reader, is mainly the work of E. Hajičová. The book has been reformulated and revised in various other respects, too. Chapter 1, and the general outline of the book, were prepared with the participation of Dr. P. Novák.

We do not claim that any particular question has been answered here in a definitive way, but the conception of a generative system based on an articulation of the semantic relation (see Section 1.3.4) may perhaps be interesting in connection with the present development of algebraic linguistics. This conception originated in 1963–1964, mainly as a reaction to the existing form of transformational description. It has not yet been possible to take the more recent impulses into account to an extent that would be adequate to their scope and theoretical significance. Only some aspects of these impulses are commented on in the relevant parts of the present book. We do not present a complete characterization of a system that could be regarded as a counterpart to the new version of transformational grammar. We have simply tried to formulate a conception that can serve as a starting point for the development of a new alternative.

Some features in the development of transformational grammar would seem to indicate that the chosen line of investigation is not unjustified. One of these indications has been Chomsky's critical approach to such issues connected with the behavioristic approach to language as the search for a mechanical procedure that would construct a grammar solely on the basis of a corpus of texts; distinguishing performance and competence, Chomsky, in a sense, advanced new support for European trends in structural linguistics against American descriptivism. The change worked on the framework of transformational grammar in 1964—the inclusion of a semantic component and the statement that transformations do not change meaning and should not be called on to account for the recursive properties of language—can be regarded as another step in this direction. Finally, if suggestions have been made recently pointing to a possible generative form for the semantic component and to a new treatment of the relation between semantic interpretation and syntactic deep structure, we might take this as fresh confirmation of the usefulness of an attempt to give an explicit formulation to some ideas connected with the functional approach of the Prague School.

We wish to thank Professor D. G. Hays for his valuable comments and wise suggestions from which we have greatly benefited in the preparation of the manuscript.

Contents

1. THE APPROACH

1.1 ALGEBRAIC LINGUISTICS

Algebraic linguistics[1] has been constituted in the writings of Noam Chomsky and others as that branch of modern linguistics which aims at an explicit, formal theory (or description) of language.[2] A theory of a particular language can meet the requirements of algebraic linguistics if it is formulated as a mathematical system and if the language described by it is an interpretation of this system. The methodological significance of this branch of linguistics for theoretical linguistics as a whole lies, first of all, in its demand for a "theory of a language" to be formulated as a theory in the technical sense of this word. Such a theory can be tested as to its consistency, as to its adequacy for the language described, etc.; it can be confronted with some other theory (of the same language, of another language, of a mathematical object of some other kind). This can be done without relying on the intuition of an interpreter of the given theory, which is not possible without the said conditions being fulfilled (cf. Chomsky, 1962b).

The main principles permitting a language to be treated in this way have been formulated by Chomsky in relation to the traditional aims of grammar as two fundamental conditions which a description of a language must satisfy (Chomsky, 1961); these are reproduced here in a somewhat altered wording:

(a) the description specifies formally the given set of (grammatical) sentences of the language described;

(b) the description assigns automatically to every sentence a set of structural characteristics that are not incompatible with the intuition of speakers of the language (in particular an n-ambiguous sentence is assigned n distinct structural characteristics).

Of course, there exist other approaches, too (e.g. the so-called analytical models of Kulagina, Revzin, Marcus and others), but Chomsky's principles quoted above have proved themselves to be fruitful, and they can be regarded as a sound basis for formulating the general frame of a description of language. The questions posed by other approaches are not thereby eliminated; on the contrary, to study them in the light of principles (a) and (b) will possibly be very useful, just as it turned out to be useful to connect the wider aims of linguistic theory (including the study of linguistic universals, the relationship between acquisition of language and linguistic competence and performance, the characterization of degrees of grammaticalness, etc.) with these principles.

These main principles should be distinguished from their actual application in the form of Chomsky's transformational description, where in addition some other basic assumptions are included, as for instance:

(c) in accordance with the American linguistic tradition, immediate constituent analysis is preferred to dependency syntax, which has been used widely since the nineteenth century (e.g. in classical philology);

(d) this analysis is combined with the use of transformational rules, esp. for cases where its application was not found adequate for the description of natural languages;

(e) the description of syntax (and of grammar) is intended to be separated from that of semantics, that is, the descriptions of grammar and of semantics are linked with each other only as wholes, as distinct components of the system;

(f) the recursive properties of the description are concentrated in its syntactic base, whereas the semantic component serves only to interpret the underlying P-markers generated by the syntactic component; in the base rules, the initial symbol *S* itself is recursive.

As is well known, some of these points were not formulated until 1964, when the new form of transformational description was set up. But the main principles (a), (b) have remained without change. This leads us to assume that those principles do not necessarily imply a unique form of generative description, that is that it is possible to search for a type of description based on the above-mentioned principles, but using other means of concretization than such as (c) to (f).

This possibility is made even more desirable by the fact that several points of the transformational conception are still under discussion. In our opinion, the most urgent of these uncertainties is that the representation of a sentence on the level of semantic interpretation (as characterized by Katz, 1964, 1966a, and by Katz-Postal, 1964) has no specific syntactic structure of its own (see Weinreich, 1966, and Sgall, 1967b).[3] Thus it is not clear whether Curry's (1961) requirement that a distinction be made between tectogrammatics (i.e., syntactic relations proper) and phenogrammatics (the means of realizing those relations) is fully met. If deep structure is viewed as tectogrammatics, then its lexical units should have another form, not including a sequence of phonemes.

We assume, therefore, that it is a reasonable task to formulate an alternative type of generative description which abandons at least some of points (c) to (f) and is based, instead, on other empirical assumptions. We have been trying to set up such an alternative, using ideas developed in the European linguistic tradition, such as dependency syntax and a gradual relation between form and function (elaborated, without an explicit formulation, by the Prague School of structural linguistics; cf. Section 1.3.2).

1.2 THE OBJECTIVE OF THIS BOOK

Our alternative type of generative description is still far from being completely formulated. The aim of this book is to present its basic assumptions and to show, in general, that it is worth while to search for a type of description that is not transformational (at least in the classical sense of this word, based on a certain form of rules), but that is in a sense stronger than taxonomic descriptions, since it has at least two distinct levels of sentence structure (i.e. it assigns more than one syntactic representation to every non-ambiguous sentence), and that is specific enough. We try (by way of experiment) to formulate explicitly an assumption (Section 1.3.4), which is founded on presuppositions stated and exemplified—without a systematic elaboration—in the linguistic tradition.

We assume that a description of this type can be formulated in such a way that Chomsky's conditions (a) and (b) are respected. For the time being, we have only a preliminary sketch of the formal properties of such systems and a framework of a description of the Czech language in this form. As the illustrations presented here in Chapters 3 and 6 show,[4] this description does not fulfil condition (a), since it does not exclude some combinations of lexical and other units that do not occur in grammatical Czech sentences; on the other hand, it fails to generate some sentences in all possible variants of their word order. A formulation generating only the grammatical sentences is possible without changes of the general formal properties of the description, but with a large number of symbols (including a loss of generality and of descriptive adequacy); we encounter here problems similar to those of Chomsky's subcategorization (see Chapter 3 for examples and Section 4.1.3 for possible ways for their future solution). A description generating all the variants of Czech word order has to face other problems (see Section 3.2, Section 4.1.2, and, for some suggestions, Sgall, 1967c).

This type of description is in certain respects very close to Lamb's stratificational linguistics (see Section 2.1.5). We do not call it stratificational, since some of the main formal properties of Lamb's model (as far as we can judge from the literature available thus far) are not shared by our description: for example the symbol is not erased or altered by the application of realizational rules (so that it can serve, in this form, for later reference—see Hockett, 1966, p. 221), but this is not the case in our system. Moreover the number of levels (strata), and, to a certain extent, the structure of some of them, are also different.[5]

In any case, the system proposed here—in common with Lamb's system—belongs to that of the two "major avenues" of generative research (Hays, 1964) combining several devices equivalent to context-free grammars in a sequence, generating by the first component a certain representation for every sentence of the language described. But the transformational description has now (after the incorporation of a semantic component and after the transfer of the recursive properties from the transformational part of the grammar to its base) many properties in common with a stratificational one (if the latter is formulated explicitly as a generative device): The set of all sentences is no longer built up in two steps (first the kernel, then the transformational extension), and if it were possible now to formulate a generative semantics,[6] then even the transformational description would have the form of a sequence of devices.

A new common basis for the confrontation of the types of description already mentioned (and, in fact, of others) can, perhaps, be found in the direction shown recently by Hockett (1966), but we have not yet been able to make full use of this possibility here. It is not yet evident whether this basis of confrontation is specific enough to make a characterization of the individual approaches possible.

1.3 THE SEMANTIC RELATION AND THE LEVELS OF LINGUISTIC DESCRIPTION

1.3.1 THE SEMANTIC RELATION

Any natural language is a system of signs, that is, a semantic system. The study of syntactic relations within language (in the sense of Carnap, Morris, etc.) is of course an inevitable task of linguistics. But it is inevitable just as a prerequisite for the analysis of the semantic relation.

To make these theses clearer (and perhaps more acceptable) let us include here a short discussion of the terms "sign" and "semantic relation."

Ferdinand de Saussure (1916) uses the term "sign" (*signe*) in a special sense, namely as a name for "the combination of a concept and a sound-image" (see p. 67); for these components of the sign he uses then the terms *signifié* and *signifiant*, respectively. Saussure does not speak of a relation, but it is obvious that the question "Is this a sign?"[7] can be answered positively only if "this" refers to an element of a certain set of pairs. Using the modern terminology, we can speak then of a binary relation and call it the semantic relation or the relation of sign. As the set of "notions" and that of "sound-images" probably are to be considered disjoint (for a notion of sound-image is not a sound-image itself, and *vice versa*), this relation is unsymmetric and irreflexive (and, of course, intransitive; cf. Hockett, 1966, p. 171, for these terms).

Charles S. Peirce, in his conception of the sign, works—as is well known—with a triadic relation (of Sign, Object, and Interpretant). Moreover, he says (cf. Peirce, 1940, p. 99) that it is a genuine triadic relation, not a combination of dyadic ones. But, nevertheless, several lines further on he himself speaks about a relation between "$First_1$" (i.e., Sign) and "$Second_1$" (Object); this relation—clearly dyadic or binary—is, according to Peirce, the $Object_2$, if confronted with the Interpretant ("$Third_1$") as with a $Sign_2$. The notion of the Interpretant (or Third)—as well as its relation to the Sign and Object—has not been formulated clearly in the work of Peirce (cf. Morris, 1946, esp. p. 289). We assume that it is more legitimate to consider the Interpretant (with de Saussure, Morris, Carnap, and others) as belonging to another layer, so that the relation of the remaining two units can be studied with the exclusion of the Interpretant. We are aware that Peirce's Sign and Object cannot be identified in all respects with de Saussure's *signifiant* and *signifié*, respectively.[8] But, considering the discrepancies as inessential for our discussion, we may regard a binary relation—in Hjelmslev's terminology it is the relation between a unit of content and a corresponding unit of expression—with the said properties as a relatively safe background for the analysis of notions such as "sign" and "semantics." (As to the "units" mentioned here, see Section 2.1.)

If we want to specify further properties of that relation, or of the corresponding operations (i.e., of the mapping of *C* onto *E*, and of the mapping of *E* onto *C*, where *C* denotes the set of units of content, and *E* denotes the set of units of expression), we have to take into consideration the notion of asymmetrical dualism of Karcevskij (1929), that is, of synonymy (paraphrase, etc.) and homonymy (polysemy, ambiguity). In the general case there are several units of *E* that correspond to a given unit of *C*—under the sign relation and operations—and several units of *C* which correspond to a given unit of *E*. So we have only a many-to-many relation, and the mappings are general ones.

In accordance with many other linguists belonging to various trends, we assume that the semantic relation (or the corresponding general mappings) must be accounted for by any theory of language deserving this name. As Katz (1967, p. 125) writes, the basic problem of (the Chomskyan) linguistic theory is "to explicate the abstract form of the knowledge that makes a speaker competent to communicate in his language," and the solution of this problem takes "the form of a model which shows how the rules of particular linguistic descriptions pair a phonetic representation of any appropriate acoustic signal with its proper semantic interpretation." Similar views, connected with other theoretical frameworks and terminologies, can be found for example in Lamb (1964a), Mel'chuk (1967), Apresjan (1967, p. 9), Zawadowski (1967). We would like to show in the next section that one of the sources of a systematic study of the semantic relation can be seen in the standpoints of some members of the classical period of the Prague School.

1.3.2 FORM AND FUNCTION IN THE PRAGUE SCHOOL

One of the characteristic aspects of the Prague School has been to regard meaning as an object of linguistic study. The units of meaning, the relations between them, and the relations of these units to the units of form (expression) are—according to the views of this school—an inherent part of the structure (system) of language (cf. Skalička, 1948). In the writings of some of the members of the Prague School we find also a certain conception of the relation between meaning (function) and form (for some ideas, see Mathesius, 1924, 1929; for a short general formulation, Havránek, 1940; a specific treatment in that line is given by Trnka, 1953–1954, 1964): the relation of form and function is handled here as a gradual one, which can be found between the sound and the phoneme, between the phonological form and the morphemic function of a morpheme, between morphemic and syntactic units, or between some other items. A subtle analysis of some aspects of the relation in question as well as a specification of various types of oppositions connected with it is presented by Hořejší (1961). As Skalička (1935) has pointed out, it is not possible to treat separately the description of function (meaning) on the one hand, and that of form on the other (cf. his treatment of such units as the morpheme and the seme, *op. cit.*, p. 15).

The endeavour after an insight into the meanings and functions of language units has been often characterized as (one aspect of) the so-called functional approach (functionalism) of the Prague School (e.g. Mathesius, 1936). Certainly, the functional approach of this school comprises several (related but distinct) principles (cf. Novák and Sgall, 1968),[9] but the question is whether the above-mentioned aspect concerns the method, or rather the scope of the object of linguistic study. Among these principles, the least abiding was, as it has turned out, the teleological, which in linguistics probably consisted in a hypostasis connected with the incontestable purposive impulse of the use of language; moreover, the questions of the source (the "control unit") and of the mechanism of regulation (when speaking of a "role" of a subsystem or of its "influence" on other subsystems, etc.) were overlooked, and, finally, the purposive and the intentional (conscious) characters of behaviour were not properly distinguished (see Novák and Sgall, 1962, p. 32). In abandoning the principle of teleology, we need not relinquish the conception of the relation of form and function (meaning).

Another aspect of this conception that is of great importance for our approach (even though we have not yet been able to make full use of it in this book) is the notion of a certain hierarchy of the units of language, be they units of form or units of function. This hierarchy has been analyzed especially in the work of Kuryłowicz (1935, 1956, 1960, 1964), where his notions of primary and secondary functions and of basic and founded forms are elaborated and illustrated.

As is well known, several approaches that are very near to the treatment of the relation of form and function as a gradual one have been developed more recently by other scholars; besides Lamb's stratificational linguistics, see Ivanov (1961), Revzin (1961), and Fitialov (1961).

An attempt to formulate this view in an axiomatic system was made by Nebeský and Sgall (1962); there the generative approach was not applied, and a relatively strong idealization of certain conditions (such as the resolving of ambiguities by context and situation) was admitted. Therefore, a thorough confrontation of the axioms then formulated with the form of the system proposed here is a rather complicated task. It is closely related with the more general task of confronting the generative approach with the so-called analytical (or set theoretical) models mentioned in Section 1.1. (The first such model, as far as we know, was suggested by Bar-Hillel, 1950; but cf. also his more recent views in Bar-Hillel, 1964, p. 3.) The authors are convinced that such a confrontation would be highly stimulating for both approaches, but do not attempt it in this book.

1.3.3 LEVELS OF THE LANGUAGE SYSTEM

A more or less vague notion of "level" as a subsystem of the system of language is present perhaps in every serious attempt at the description of language. This is mainly due to the effort towards a systematic or relatively simple description (see for instance Chomsky, 1957, Section 3.1). In traditional linguistics, and also in the Prague School, no explicit definition of this notion has been presented, and Prague scholars have reached no agreement as to the number of levels.[10] Hjelmslev's system contains only two levels, that of content (*le plan du contenu*) and that of expression (*le plan de l'expression*). But, in this case, the levels can be identified with both the sets of units between which the semantic relation holds (cf. Section 1.3.1). Even by distinguishing "substance" and "form" within each level (which was, in fact, done by de Saussure's specification of *signifié* and *signifiant*) one has no opportunity to characterize clearly, without additional means, the distinctions between, say, nominative case, subject, and actor, or between units of systematic phonetics (sounds), phonology (phonemes and their variants, or allophones), and morphophonemics.[11] Many linguists use more than two levels in their linguistic descriptions, even if they regard both Hjelmslev's "plans" as dominating, in some sense, the hierarchy of the system of levels.

The first formal definition of the notion of linguistic level was given by Chomsky in his dissertation (1955, Chapter 2). If we interpret his formulations properly, the following three basic points associated with the notion of level can be stated that are not confined to the specific form of transformational grammar:

(1) There is a mathematical system, that is, the means to represent a sentence on the given level (with Chomsky, this system is a concatenation algebra, as he works with representations of sentences in the form of strings; but it is possible to use other forms, too, e.g. graphs or networks—cf. Lamb, 1964a, Hockett, 1966, Sgall, 1966a, 1967c).

(2) At each level, the set of strings (graphs etc.) defined by the system mentioned in (1) contains at least one representation of every sentence of the language described. (In this point we differ from Chomsky, 1955, but perhaps not from the more recent development of his theory).

(3) The relations of each level to other levels are defined.

If these points are considered essential, it is only a matter of terminology whether the term "level" should be used as the name of the mathematical system (algebra) mentioned in (1), or as the name of the set (2) of sentence representations specified by this system. Chomsky prefers the first alternative but this prevents formulations such as "this level contains n representations of sentence a" or "all strings that are members of level A can be transduced to level B by this procedure", formulations which seem quite harmless and even useful. Thus we use the term level in the second sense, assuming, of course, that it is a set specified by a system of the type mentioned in (1).

Points (1) to (3), as well as principles (a) and (b) dealt with in Section 1.1, call for some further remarks. If the description is adequate, then each of its levels contains exactly one representation of every non-ambiguous sentence; for each ambiguous sentence, there is at least one level with two or more representations of that sentence, and for every set of mutually synonymous sentences there is at least one level in the description where the members of the set have a common representation. In neither case can the phonetic level belong to the set from which "at least one level" may be chosen; mostly the semantic interpretation (or whatever the "level of meaning" may be called) belongs to it (though there are more complicated cases, too, cf. the examples given at the end of Section 2.1.4). This leads to the assumption that there is a certain hierarchy or some kind of ordering of levels, which can be evaluated linguistically by means of the semantic relation (see Section 1.3.1 concerning this relation and its connection with asymmetrical dualism, i.e. homonymy and synonymy, and Section 1.3.4 for our view on the hierarchy).

But in the theory of transformational descriptions these implications are not made explicit, and the linguistic evaluation of the relations between levels remains somewhat unclear. The necessity of working with different levels is stated in several places (e.g. in Chomsky, 1957, pp. 18, 24), and the levels are characterized negatively in that higher levels are not "literally constructed out of lower level elements" (*op. cit.*, p. 59). The relations between levels are characterized by formulations such as "Notice that in this view one major function of the transformational rules is to convert an abstract deep structure that expresses the content of a sentence into a fairly concrete surface structure that indicates its form" (Chomsky, 1965, p. 136). But what are the meanings of the words "express" and "indicate" here? Is the meaning of "express" connected with the relation of "content" and "expression"?

Another point to be decided is: which of the two ways of ordering of levels should be considered fundamental for their linguistic evaluation—that based on the order "deep structure—surface structure—phonemics—phonetics," or that conditioned by the internal structure of levels? (See Chomsky, 1955, where the transformational level is considered, in a certain sense, as the highest, since it operates with the strongest mathematical means, i.e., since T-markers are mathematical objects of greater complexity than P-markers.) The answer is perhaps that in the new form of transformational descriptions no T-markers are needed any more, and the structural characterization of the representation of the sentence on the level of surface structure can use simpler means than those of its deep structure.

In any case, it seems clear that even in the theory of transformational description it is preferable to choose—out of the two ways of ordering—that hierarchy of levels which is consistent with the semantic relation. We can say that the development of the transformational description leads, in this respect, to a decisive convergence with the stratificational and similar types of descriptions (where this interpretation of the hierarchy of levels was present, without, of course, a formally elaborated formulation). We shall examine in the next section the nature of the relationship between the hierarchy of levels and the semantic relation.

1.3.4 THE HIERARCHY OF LEVELS AS AN ARTICULATION OF THE SEMANTIC RELATION

Our conception of the semantic relation (cf. Section 1.3.1) leads to the following assumption (perhaps it may be called a hypothesis, but we do not mean by this that its testability is clearer than that of other linguistic assumptions; we are aware that there are many open questions, concerning, first of all, the notion of a semantic representation of a sentence; some of them will be pointed out later):

Given the semantic relation (and both the sets of sentence representations for which this relation is defined), it is possible to formulate a procedure translating each element of the set of semantic representations of sentences into at least one element of the set of phonetic representations of sentences, in such a manner that

(a) the operation of translation defined by this procedure is a general (many-to-many) mapping of the set of semantic representations onto the set of phonetic representations;

(b) a representation r is mapped (translated) into a representation q if and only if r and q are representations of the same sentence (where r is an element of the set of semantic representations, and q is an element of the set of phonetic representations of sentences);

(c) the whole procedure can be specified in the form of a universal Turing machine or of a transducer equivalent to it (where "equivalent" is used for two types of devices whose sets of input languages are identical, and so are their sets of output languages);

(d) the operation of translation can be divided into several steps so that the input language of the device (transducer) performing the first step is identical with the set of semantic representations, and the output language of the device performing the i-th step ($1 \leqslant i \leqslant n-1$, where n is the number of steps) is a subset of the input language of the device performing the $(i+1)$-th step, and the output language of the device performing the n-th step contains the set of phonetic representations of sentences as a subset; each transducer maps every representation of a given sentence into a representation of the same sentence;

(e) each of the devices (transducers) involved in (d) belongs to a type that is specific enough to be mathematically–and thus also linguistically–interesting.

Alternatively, point (d) can be stated in a stronger form, namely with the output language of the i-th transducer identical to the input language of the $(i+1)$-th; then the output language of the n-th transducer would be identical with the set of all phonetic representations (whereas in (d) there holds only inclusion instead of identity); on this alternative between the stronger and weaker forms of the assumption, see Section 2.2.5.

Taking this assumption (in its stronger or weaker form), we can speak about an articulation of the operation of translation between the two sets mentioned above. If we regard the pair formed by a certain element of the set of semantic representations and one of its images in the set of all phonetic representations as an element of the semantic relation (see Section 1.3.1), and if we now consider the output (or input) language of any of the devices mentioned in (d) as a level, we can say that the semantic relation itself is articulated, in this type of description, into relations each of which holds between two adjacent levels.

With this articulation of the semantic relation the hierarchy (or ordering) of levels in a description allows for a more direct linguistic evaluation, connected with the relativization of the relation of "form" and "function" that we find in the writings of Prague and other scholars (cf. Section 1.3.2).

Our assumption, of course, cannot be directly proved, and even in the future its empirical verification can be only very incomplete. The speaker's (and hearer's) linguistic competence is in a sense a "black box" whose internal structure can be studied only indirectly, on the basis of its "output," which is the only thing accessible for our direct knowledge. (And even here, the attribute "direct" has to be taken in a relative sense.) Therefore there is a danger of hypostasis if we speak of a sequence of levels, since the "inner" (i-th) ones (with $2 \leqslant i \leqslant n$, n as above) are only assumed by the assumption, whereas the first and the last, that is $(n+1)$-th, are "more granted" (of course with different degrees of accessibility). But there is no other possibility than to search for a relatively simple description of the structure of the "black box" that would be adequate to the known properties of its output (and also to our knowledge of the "input," derived from logic and psychology). Simplicity of description—for which there are no explicit criteria—is not only a matter of "aesthetics," but of pragmatic considerations (cf. Oettinger, 1961) as well; in this case, we have to assume—as Prof. Kuryłowicz suggested in his lectures—that, after many thousands of years of development of natural languages, the organization of the linguistic competence of their users has become relatively effective.

The relation between a unit of a certain level and the corresponding unit of the next lower level[12] is called realization here (cf. Trnka, 1958, Lamb, 1964b). We are aware that there are various distinctions between, say, the realization of units of the first level by units of the second, and the realization of units of the second level by those of the third. Each level has its own syntax, that is, its own restrictions on possible combinations of units. With the weaker alternative of our assumption, the syntax of a level could be described, perhaps, by the input language of the corresponding transducer, whereas the output language of the preceding transducer is only a proper subset, consisting of the strings having corresponding strings at the preceding level; cf. now also Hockett (1966, p. 299). Some pairs of adjacent levels have more of the structure of their units in common (at least in our form of the description;

cf. Section 2.1) than others, and probably also the asymmetrical dualism between different levels undergoes different restrictions.

It is not certain, of course, whether such an articulation of the operation assigning a set of phonetic representations to each semantic representation of a sentence should consist of such "complete" levels as we are assuming here (cf. point (2) in Section 1.3.3); another possibility is to formulate only a set of rules whose successive application would not specify any intermediate levels (as sets of strings having some interesting formal properties in common). However, what is known about such domains as phonetics, phonemics, and morphemics leads to the assumption that for the "higher" levels also it might be useful to divide the set of rules into subsets conceivable as rules of transducing devices specifying the levels. Even so, there are certainly many units of various kinds that need not be changed if contained in a representation of a sentence that is "transduced" to the next level by such a device. (This concerns most of the so-called suffixes; cf. Section 2.1.3.)

There is yet another question, formulated by Householder (1962), which can be referred to briefly as the irreversibility of the sequence of levels: it is easy to imagine two languages that coincide in their sets of semantic interpretations of sentences (i.e. in the first level), while they diverge widely in their phonetic realizations; but the reverse—the possibility of the same set of (phonetic representations of) sentences corresponding to two distinct sets of semantic interpretations—is hard to conceive. In any case, the first (tectogrammatical) levels of different languages are relatively close to each other (cf. Curry, 1961), and we assume it natural to take this end of the sequence of levels as the "starting point" of the description, and not the other one.

NOTES

1. See Bar-Hillel, 1964, pp. 185–187, for this term and for a short account of the background and beginnings of the discipline, including the share of logicians, who paved the way for a systematic use of formal means in linguistic description.
2. Here the term "language" is used not for a set of sentences (as by Chomsky), but for the natural language system which is the object of linguistic description (cf. Schnelle, 1963). Only when speaking about a formal language (e.g. an input language of an automaton), is this term used in the former sense.
3. Katz (1966a, 1967) makes some suggestions showing a way of overcoming this inadequacy; a systematic elaboration of the syntax of his semantic interpretations would mean, of course, that the criticism by Weinreich and others is overcome.
4. The Czech examples are chosen in such a way that the structure of most of them is quite parallel in the relevant points to that of the accompanying translations (where the English translation is not apt for this purpose, a German or Russian one is added).
5. Some of the main features of our system have been formulated independently of Lamb's stratificational linguistics (cf. Sgall, 1963, for the hierarchy or sequence of levels), but we should like to acknowledge the influence his ideas offered during our work.
6. In this case the semantic component would have the form of a device enumerating constructively the set of all semantic interpretations of sentences. With regard to other components, there are two possibilities: (1) there would be a transducing component having the above set as (a subset of) its input language and the set of deep structure representations as (a subset of) its output language; (2) both these sets could be identified,

that is, deep structure would be abandoned as a special level, as suggested by Lakoff and Ross (1967).

7. His terminological value of "sign", as he remarks, is not identical with the meaning of this word in "current usage," but he found no better term. In this case the question whether the *signifié* should or should not be "included" in the sign appears primarily as a matter of terminology. If we use the term "sign" in the sense of de Saussure (as opposed to many previous scholars, be it Peirce or, say, Fortunatov), we have to understand it just as a name for the pair of *signifiant* (called sign by those other scholars) and *signifié*. Another question is, whether we need a name for this pair.
8. Cf. now Godel (1966, pp. 486f) for an analysis of de Saussure's *signifié*.
9. Cf. Garvin (1964, pp. 148–152) for an operational account of a certain aspect of Prague functionalism.
10. A short account of the development of the notion of level within the Prague School was given in Hořejší's study quoted above.
11. Cf. Lamb (1966c, pp. 567f) for a more thorough statement of similar reasoning in these lines.
12. Formally, we assume that a relation R is defined whose domain is level A and whose range is level B, both taken as sets of strings at least some of which are representations of sentences. If $(a, b) \in R$, where $a \in A$ and $b \in B$, we shall say that a is realized by b; we shall sometimes speak informally of the relation between levels A and B, or between their units. However, in linguistic writings one usually speaks of the relation of realization between smaller units, too (e.g. of morphs realizing morphemes, etc.), since in the typical cases strings such as a, b above can be subdivided into such smaller units; but this cannot be done in a simple way for all elements of the levels (cf. for instance cases with Lamb's horizontal asymmetry; further problems arise from contextual restrictions concerning realization in this sense of the word). Here and in Section 2.1 we also adopt this inexact usage, but we are aware that a formal treatment of such smaller units should be based on a generative description (see e.g. Bierwisch, 1962).

2. THE FORM OF THE DESCRIPTION

2.1 INFORMAL ACCOUNT

2.1.1 THE LEVELS AND TRADITIONAL LINGUISTICS

In traditional and structural linguistics (including, especially, the Prague School) language is studied in terms of such levels as phonetics, phonology, morphemics, the syntax of the sentence and the semantic structure of the sentence. The degree of explicitness with which the individual levels have been elaborated varies to a considerable extent and only a few points have been settled with general agreement. Nevertheless, many basic notions concerning such levels have been verified in a way, in that they have been used for many decades or even centuries in descriptions of languages that have served various purposes.

We are aware, of course, that these descriptions have been used mainly in a few types of applications, with a more or less "pedagogical" orientation, so that their basic notions have to be re-examined from the viewpoint of theoretical linguistics. Certainly, the tradition of schoolroom linguistics (differing in different countries), the properties of the mother tongue, and the connection with various applications tend to influence the theory in many respects. But we do not want to abandon any of the previous results just because of the mere difference between the traditional bases of language teaching in Czech and American high schools. We should like to try to make use of the results of traditional linguistics (as far as we are able to account for them), departing from them only in cases where this is clearly motivated.

An attempt to use the traditional concepts in the framework of an explicit description can be conceived—more or less—as a critical analysis of them. It necessarily reveals various inadequacies of the pre-systematic conception; to remove their consequences that hinder attempts at a formal elaboration of the conception, it may even be necessary to change some of the basic formal properties of the framework initially chosen.

Among the traditional concepts, those concerning the two levels of syntactic and semantic structure of the sentence are most lacking in general agreement. Therefore it may be useful to add some remarks concerning those classical conceptions of these two levels that have been chosen as the empirical background of the type of description proposed in this book.

With respect to the syntactic structure of the sentence, the classical dependency syntax has been used generally as a part of the description of Slavonic languages; for the Czech language, its most detailed presentation has been given by Šmilauer (1947, 1957). As to the individual units of this level, our description is based on his analysis, except for cases where there are strong arguments for another solution. As to the general standpoint, the dependency relation is considered to be the relation between the two members of the syntagm; the syntagm is a pair of syntactic words (cf. Section 2.1.3 concerning this term), one of which (the governor) "stands for" the whole pair in its "outer relations" (cf. Kuryłowicz, 1948). The relations of one syntagm to other words within a sentence are realized by the same means as the relations of the governor (i.e., the expanded, modified member) of the syntagm to other words. We suppose this criterion to be decisive for the determination of the governing member of the syntagm (i.e., of the direction of the dependency relation) even in cases where the arrangement of the means itself would imply the opposite direction. Therefore in the predicative syntagm the predicate is regarded as the governor and the subject as the dependent, since it is the predicate which stands for the whole predicative syntagm with respect both to the dependents (esp. to the adverbials) and to the governor (i.e., to the governing clause). Further advantages of this treatment of the predicative syntagm are presented by Tesnière (1959), and—as regards formal characterization—by Fitialov (1962). Another formal treatment of the predicative relation is possible, namely that of the mutual dependency of the two members; this is the approach adopted by Revzin (1961).

From the point of view of the dependency relation, there is no difference between a member's modifying the whole syntagm and its modifying its governor only. It is true that there are certain restrictions with respect to word order; but when the dependents are on different sides of the governor, the syntactic structure of the sentence does not make it possible to decide which of them is more closely connected to the governor.[1] For instance, in a sentence such as *Yesterday I read this book with great delight*, we can undoubtedly claim that the verb (with its object) is modified by two adverbials, but the syntactic structure of this sentence does not show whether one of these adverbials is more closely connected to the verb than the other.

As has been stated in Section 1.3.2, some members of the Prague School regard the semantic structure of the sentence as a level of its own, whose units are "functions" or "meanings" of the units of the syntactic (or grammatical) structure of the sentence. In this sense Mathesius (1924, 1929) wrote about the relation between subject and actor. Later Dokulil and Daneš (1958) presented a deep analysis of various aspects of the relationship between the two levels of sentence structure. In their conception the content of the sentence (utterance, or some larger or smaller units) is characterized as consisting in "the conceptual structure, without being mediated by the language form" (p. 240), and is contrasted with the meaning of a grammatical unit, understood as "a point of intersection of conceptual contents (as a reflection of reality) and of the organizing principle of the sentence structure" (p. 240).

We attempt to apply Dokulil and Daneš's general concepts in our elaboration of the semantic structure of the sentence (where meaning but not content should be included), though we depart from them in the evaluation of certain individual units; first of all, such units as actor, action, and goal are regarded in our conception not as units of mere content, but as units of meaning.

Let us take the following sentences:

Měsíc osvětluje krajinu svými paprsky (*The Moon lights up the countryside with its beams*)
Voda zaplavila louku (*The water flooded the meadow*)
Londýn převyšuje Glasgow rozlohou a počtem obyvatel (*London exceeds Glasgow in size and population*)
Auto ho srazilo předními koly (*The car knocked him down with its front wheels*)
Padající kámen ho zasáhl svým ostrým koncem (*The falling stone struck him with its sharp edge*)

In these sentences the status of the first member as an actor[2] certainly is not given only by a reflection of reality in the conceptual structure, but is mediated by the language form. In this respect, we follow here Skalička, who explains the extended validity of the sentence pattern actor–action (–goal) by the "anthropocentric" nature of syntax (which apparently is connected with the conditions under which the structure of the sentence originated); this pattern is fully suitable for sentences referring to some human action, but it also underlies many other sentences, as for example *The sun is shining. This shows the truth* (cf. Skalička, 1962). If we regard the actor as realized by subject, primarily, we differ from Chomsky (1957, Section 9.2.7) just in that "actor" is, in our terminology, a unit of meaning conceived as dependent on grammar (only the content being independent of it).

A more detailed account of the relationship between the syntactic and semantic levels (and also with respect to functional sentence perspective—cf. Section 4.2.1 below) is given by Daneš in his recent studies (1963, 1964a, 1964b). The objective of the first is the notion of the sentence (as a unit belonging to the language system, not as part of a text) and the characteristics of the sentence at the level of its grammatical structure. His second study gives an analysis of the semantic structure of the sentence and of the organization of the utterance (functional sentence perspective) and points out an inconsistency in distinguishing "grammatical" and "semantic" relations between constituents of a sentence as presented by Chomsky. In his third study, Daneš attempts an account of the individual units of the grammatical structure of the sentence with respect to the corresponding types of homonymy. Some of his examples show, in our opinion, a homonymy between the level of grammatical sentence structure and the level of its semantic structure: *Všichni tomu nevěřili.* (*All of them did not believe it.* or *Not all of them believed it.*) *Kritika polského delegáta byla správná.* (*The criticism of the Polish delegate was true.* or *The criticism by the Polish delegate*...) *Zahlédli ji až při odchodu z divadla.* (*They saw her at the time of leaving the theatre.* i.e. *when she, or they*, or *all the people were leaving the theatre.*) According to our conception (which we by no means suppose to be the only one possible) each of the cited sentences has a single representation on the level of grammatical structure, but several distinct representations on the level of semantic structure. So we may speak of homonymy between the representations of this sentence on the two levels; that means there is a relation of function and form between them. Since we suppose the distinction between the levels of semantic and syntactic structures of the sentence to be essentially conformable to Curry's (1961) distinction between tectogrammatics and phenogrammatics, we call them the tectogrammatical and the phenogrammatical level, respectively.

Of course, the parallelism between the two levels is far from complete[3] (as has been illustrated by the examples of homonymy cited above), but the discrepancies involved are similar to those between any other pair of adjacent levels, and they do not prevent treatment of the relation between the two levels in the manner suggested above (cf. also Novák, 1966a).

The investigation of the higher levels of the language system is relatively difficult, since they are not open to direct observation, and there remain many points that have not yet been studied empirically in a systematic way. In the present book, we confine ourselves to a few questions about meaning, and we do not try to investigate whether its relationship to content (both terms used in the sense of Dokulil and Daneš) can be understood as another stage of the relation of form to function (realization), again with asymmetrical dualism, or whether more such stages are to be distinguished. We assume that with the help of a clearer—if only tentative—characterization of the semantic structure of the sentence it will be possible to find a more revealing formulation of questions concerning still higher levels.

2.1.2 REMARKS ON MORPHEMICS

Before giving an account of the generative system itself, we must discuss what kinds of units should be used and what relationships between them should be assumed. Therefore we present here first of all some considerations on the system of levels and their units, based on the descriptive approach, in Chomsky's terminology (i.e. without a generative approach, which will be applied in Section 2.2). We begin our discussion with morphemics and lower levels, since the questions involved there have already been elucidated to a relatively high degree.

In recent years, many linguists have devoted their studies to a systematic analysis of the relation of realization and also of the syntactic relations at individual levels. These studies concern both the formal characterization of these relations in a certain part of the language system (Fitialov's morphemic analysis, 1961) and a more general program of analysis (e.g. Ivanov, 1961), or a detailed discussion of the basic notions (Hockett, 1961). The first attempt to model the whole system of language levels connected by the realization relation was made by Lamb (1964a, 1964b, 1966b).

We accept the analysis of the notion of morpheme given by Hockett, considering for instance the forms *go*/*went*, *be*/*are* to be characteristic examples of a single morpheme (more exactly, of two morphs corresponding to a single lexical morpheme). According to this conception a morpheme is not a string (or a sequence) of morphophonemes. In such cases as *calf/calv(es)* the morpheme could be understood in this way, but the former examples show that this treatment is not general enough, failing to account for all cases that should be covered by the notion of morpheme.

In Hockett's work several possible approaches to the relation between phoneme and morpheme are illustrated by two diagrams (Figures 1 and 2). The first exemplifies two possible methods of relating morphemes and phonemes:

(a) the relation is mediated by morphophonemes (go from upper left to the right and then down); the relation of morphemes to morphophonemes is symbolized by "*C*" and is read "(*is*) *composed of* (an arrangement of)" and that of morphophonemes to phonemes is symbolized by "*R*" and may be read "(*is*) *represented by*";[4]

(b) the relation is mediated by morphs (go first down and then to the right); a morpheme *is represented* by a fixed morph and a morph *is composed* of an arrangement of zero or more phonemes.

Viewed from a certain standpoint, the two methods are equivalent (both get us from morphemes to phonemes), but the description of a language will differ according to which method is used (morphophonemes are present in conception (a) only, morphs in conception (b)).

Hockett considers method (a) to be convenient in such cases as, for instance, the German *Bund* and *Bunde* (with the morphophoneme *d/t*), method

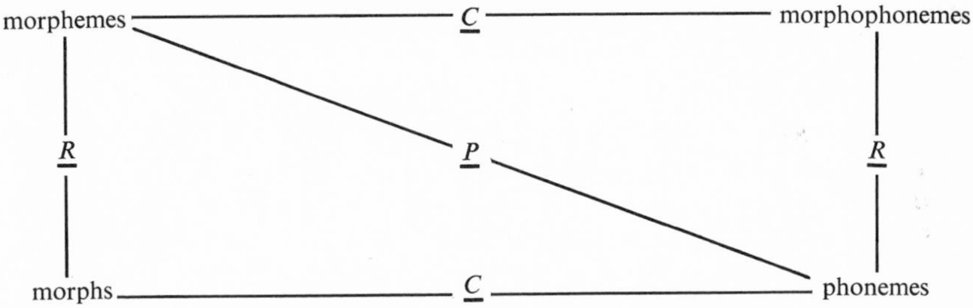

Figure 1. Morphs and Morphophonemes.

(b) being appropriate for such cases as the English *go/went* (a morpheme with two morphs).

Another approach, which is needed for more complicated examples (Hockett quotes the language Potawatomi), is illustrated by Hockett's second diagram (Figure 2). With this approach, the path proceeds from the morphemes to units representing them (as in (b) above), then to the elementary units of this (new) level, and finally—as in (a)—to the phonemes representing those elementary units.

The question must be asked whether the diagrams quoted above exclude one another or whether they are just special cases of the same type, which can be represented by a single diagram. Viewed from this aspect it is evident that both methods from the first diagram can be illustrated by the second (more

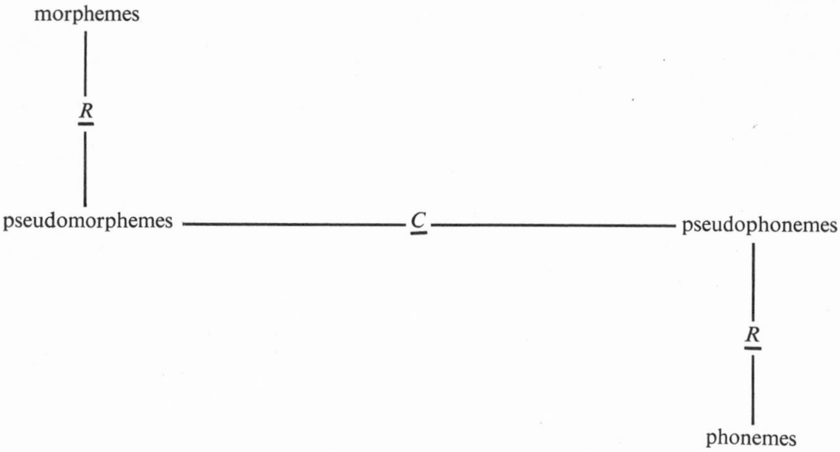

Figure 2. Pseudomorphemes and Pseudophonemes.

general) diagram as its special (extreme) cases. Thus this scheme can also be applied to those languages (or subsystems) in which one of the two relations of type *R* is reduced to a one-to-one relation, making it possible to identify either pseudomorphemes with morphemes, or pseudophonemes with phonemes. The first case would occur if the system included no suppletive morphemes, while the latter possibility would occur in a system in which there were no systematic morphophonemic alternations nor phonemic neutralizations at morpheme junctures.

Hockett supposes morphophonemes to be unjustifiable ("misfits") from the point of view of phonemics (since they cannot be defined in the terms of phonemics) and morphs to be "misfits" from the points of view of morphemics. These are his reasons for rejecting the multilevel system with relation *R*. As to this point, the method illustrated in Figure 2 might appear even less justifiable, since the pseudomorphemes and pseudophonemes are "misfits" from both the phonemic and morphemic points of view.

We do not consider it necessary to accept this argumentation. True, the units represented by phonemes cannot be defined in the terms of phonemics—just as a phoneme cannot be defined in the terms of phonetics—but this need not be considered a necessary condition. Also the standpoint of generative phonology shows that it is necessary to take account of units corresponding more or less closely to Trubeckoj's morphophonemes (cf. Halle, 1959 and Chomsky, 1962a).

Since we work only with the relations shown in Figure 2, it is possible to use the terms morphophoneme (instead of pseudophoneme) and morph (instead of pseudomorpheme), in order not to diverge unnecessarily from the current terminology. In this sense, a morph is a complex unit of the morphophonemic level, composed of morphophonemes.

Thus we achieve a simple diagram illustrating the relations at the levels lower than that of the grammatical structure of the sentence (Figure 3). In

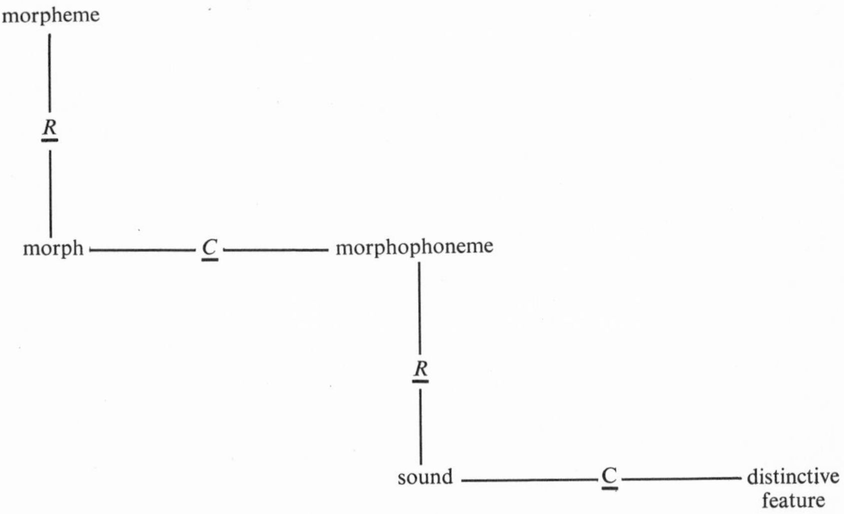

Figure 3. Main Units at the Lower Levels.

accordance with the works on generative phonology mentioned above, we do not work with the classical phonemic level, although a possibility is left for its insertion, which would bring our system in line with the views of many linguists, from the Prague School to Lamb (cf. now Vachek, 1964 and Lamb, 1966a). This question, however, is not substantial for the articulation of higher levels.

Let us turn now to the phonetic level. We regard sounds as elements of the language system, and not only as elements of an "unlimited" physiological class of sounds, as is sometimes suggested. It is evident that, for instance, the sound /ŋ/ exists in Czech as well as in English or French, although there is no corresponding phoneme (morphophoneme) in Czech; on the contrary, there is no such sound in Russian. (This standpoint is in accordance with that of generative phonology and also with other works, cf. for instance Bloch, 1941.)

At this level, sounds are regarded as complex units, composed of distinctive features. These terms are based on the traditional mode of expression, corresponding to the treatment of sound as a certain object characterized by its distinctive features. But we believe that in accordance with present-day phonemic theories (cf. esp. Jakobson, Fant, and Halle, 1952; Jakobson and Halle, 1956), it is possible to take not the sound but the distinctive feature as a primitive term; a partition of the set of distinctive features can then be defined, its elements being sets of features corresponding to the binary sets of the phonemic theory (e.g. strident–non-strident; if another phonemic theory is used, these subsets need not be binary). The sound can then be characterized by means of a set of distinctive features, such that each of its elements belongs to a different subset and each of the subsets contains some of its elements. If we define *a combination of elements from the sets* $A_1, A_2 \ldots A_n$ as a set $a_{i_1}\ a_{i_2} \ldots a_{i_n}$, where every a_{i_k} is a member of A_k (for $1 \leqslant k \leqslant n$) and all the sets A_k are mutually disjoint, then the sound as a unit of our description can be characterized as a combination of distinctive features from all elements of the partition defined in a certain phonemic theory.

The formulation presented here shows a substantial difference from that of Marcus (1963, p. 56) in one respect only, leaving aside the degree of formalization: the sound is characterized here on the basis of distinctive features, so that only one undefined primitive term is needed in a description of the type suggested, namely the elementary unit, not the complex.

We suppose that a similar situation can be envisaged at the morphemic level. Whereas in present-day American linguistics the morpheme is regarded as an elementary unit of this level, in the European tradition, especially in connection with inflecting languages, the morpheme is often considered as composed of other units. It is evident, for instance, that Russian *-ov* in *stolov* can be described as a morph, that is as a unit realizing one morpheme; this morpheme is specified usually by means of such units as genitive, plural, and others. A structural characterization of the latter kind of unit, called the seme, is given by Skalička (1935). In analytic and agglutinative languages several semes are seldom combined in the same morpheme (only in cases of so-called portmanteau-representation). If one distinguishes between morpheme and seme, a morpheme consisting of a single seme can easily be described as an extreme case of a more general situation. (Quite similarly, morphs consisting of a single morphophoneme are obviously treated as one-element sequences of morphophonemes, and no one would take a morphophoneme for a morph.)

If such types of units as case, number, gender, etc. are conceived of as sets of semes, then the morpheme is a combination of elements of those sets, for example morphemes of the Czech adjectival declension are combinations of the elements of case, number, gender, and some other sets.[5] In this treatment of the morpheme, a partition of the set of semes into subsets, some of which correspond to the types of units mentioned above, is of course presupposed. In contrast to the sound, the morpheme is a combination of elements from some members of the given partition only, not from all of them. It is possible to distinguish different kinds of morphemes according to what elements of the partition are concerned. Thus for instance, a lexical (stem) morpheme can be regarded as a combination of semes from one set only (the set of lexical semes).[6] As to the formal treatment, it is then necessary to include in every element of the partition a special "zero" seme of the given type, or to define the different types of morphemes separately (Sgall, 1960, p. 75 discusses the Czech declensional morphemes of individual word-classes); further on we assume that the latter possibility has been chosen.

The relationship existing between a preposition (as a seme) and the seme of case inside a prepositional case must be treated at the morphemic level as well, since at the phenogramatical level there is no distinction between prepositional and simple cases. In Hockett's terminology this relation is of type *C*. The corresponding complex unit is not a morpheme, for a morpheme is—as a rule—represented by a single morph.This new complex unit of the morphemic level, called a formeme in our treatment, cannot be defined on the basis of its relationship to the next lower level (it is not represented by a single morph; the preposition has a morph of its own, while the seme of case is included, together with some other semes, in another morpheme, represented by a different morph). The formeme is characterized in that it realizes a single unit from the next higher level, that is, from the phenogrammatical structure of the sentence. But even this property is not quite general, for there are cases like *in front of*, *by means of*, etc., where the whole phrase functions as a preposition. We do not attempt to give a definition of this type of unit here, supposing that some of these difficulties can be avoided if the definition is formulated within the generative system (cf. note 12 to Chapter 1). Like the morpheme, the formeme can be considered a combination of semes of certain sets.

For the purpose of this book, such relations as the combination of morphemes into words (as well as phonetic units such as syllables, breath groups, etc.) have been left aside.

Our exposition can be illustrated by the following examples of different kinds of morphemes: (a) Russian genitive-plural-neuter-noun, (b) the stem *mat'/mater'*, (c) the stem *pros/sh*. Morpheme (a) consists of four semes and is realized either by zero (*mest*) or by *-ej*(*polej*); morpheme (b) consists of a single seme and is realized by one of two different morphs; morpheme (c) consists of a single morph (whose last morphophoneme is *s/sh*).

2.1.3 THE LEVELS OF SENTENCE STRUCTURE

In proceeding from the morphemic level to the levels of sentence structure, the formemes, as units realizing units of the phenogrammatical level, can be taken as the starting point. We follow the view held by the Prague School, by Kuryłowicz and others, and we assume that the grammatical formemes realize[7] either a syntactic function, for example a sentence part (understood as a relation, not a category), or a unit of the domain of so-called "morphological semantics". For instance, the Czech or Russian accusative may realize the object (as a relation); a formeme of tense (present, preterite, etc.) may realize either the primary temporal meaning or the relative time of an action; the formeme of instrumental realizes units such as the instrument, the means, etc. Of course, there are situations in which units of both kinds are realized by a single formeme; for instance the accusative in sentences such as the Czech *Byl tam celý den* (*He stayed there the whole day*) realizes the function of an adverbial as well as the meaning of a time interval.

Alongside the two kinds of units mentioned, there is a third, namely the unit realized primarily by a lexical formeme. The lexical unit of the phenogrammatical level is not in general identical with the so-called lexical meaning. This can be shown by the examples of the verbs *to begin* and *to start*, which have at least two meanings in common (they can be illustrated by such sentences as *It is time to . . . our work. We . . . with page 30*); it might be useful to insert a unit realizing the two meanings and realized by the two stem formemes (cf. Section 2.1.6). One could speak of a single naming unit (for this term, cf. e.g. Vachek's English summary of Mathesius, 1961) realized by two different formemes and realizing two different meanings.

We shall call an elementary unit of the phenogrammatical level a tagmeme; then three kinds of tagmemes should be distinguished: the lexical tagmemes, the syntactic tagmemes, termed sentence parts, and the morphological tagmemes, termed suffixes. If compound words are—for the time being—not taken into account, a unit called the phenogrammatical (syntactic) word-form can be specified as a combination of elements from several sets, that is of one lexical tagmeme with a certain number of suffixes (whose number and types are at least partly determined by the type of the lexical tagmeme) and with at most one sentence part. A phenogrammatical word can then be characterized as a set of all phenogrammatical word-forms containing a single lexical tagmeme. The complex unit of this level (the representation of a sentence) is called a syntagmeme; as will be shown later, it can be regarded as a string and specified similarly to a formula of a calculus. So at least two relations (or operations) of type C should be distinguished at this level.

The tectogrammatical level, corresponding to the level of the semantic structure of the sentence in the terms of some members of the Prague School (cf. Section 2.1.1), has not yet been studied systematically and we can present here only a tentative sketch of its structure. There are many questions left open, which will have to be elaborated more thoroughly on the basis of detailed empirical studies. In trying to provide a preliminary starting point for this elaboration, we apply two working principles, which are based on the fact that the tectogrammatical level is meant to correspond to Dokulil and Daneš's meaning, not to content (cf. Section 2.1.1): (i) the tectogrammatical units are formulated to be as close to the phenogrammatical units as possible, so that clear reasons can be given for every difference assumed between the two levels; (ii) the number of tectogrammatical units should be as small as possible, so that clear reasons can be given for every new unit. Besides, there are other restrictions that should be overcome, for example to account for units larger than the sentence and for anaphoric phenomena where referential meaning and not only signification plays its role (cf. Palek, 1967, 1968) etc.

On this level, too, three kinds of elementary units—called semantemes—are distinguished: the lexical semantemes, the functors, and the morphological semantemes, for which the same term "suffix" is used as for the morphological tagmemes (since the formal status of morphological units is the same on both the levels).

The examples given here and in Chapters 3 and 6 illustrate only some of the most salient features of the sentence structure; we have not yet attempted to make a more detailed analysis, which would concern features that should perhaps be considered as semantic and that have not yet been systematically studied from the empirical point of view. Thus, for instance, we have studied the classification of verbs only as far as it is based on the criterion of obligatory expansion (*to meet somebody*, *to aim at something*, *to find o. s. somewhere*, etc.); nouns and adjectives have not been subdivided at all. (These terms refer here to the so-called semantic word-classes; this notion will be discussed below). A more detailed classification is, however, possible within the general framework of the system proposed here; this would lead to a large number of symbols and rules in a context-free grammar, but it is possible to find a solution using a system weakly equivalent to a context-free grammar (see Section 4.1.3).

As to types of expansions of verbs, many traditional attempts at classification are known that could be supposed relevant for the semantic structure of the sentence (e.g. the bearer of an action or that of a quality are distinguished from the actor, the "inner object" from other types of goal, etc.). It will be necessary, however, to investigate thoroughly which of these distinctions belong to the meaning in the sense of Section 2.1.1 and which are only a matter of the extra-linguistic content: in a sentence such as *He lived a rich life* the "inner object" itself (its head) does not add any new information to that conveyed by the verb, but it is far from clear whether this fact should be provided for by distinguishing this type of relationship between the verb and the noun as a special syntactic relation; perhaps it is only a matter of semantic coincidence of two lexical units. Another similar question is that of "types of goal" as to their being changed, caused, destroyed, etc. by the given action (now cf. e.g. Lakoff and Ross, 1967).

In any case, we do not suppose that such notions as subject and object are sufficient for the tectogrammatical level (as has recently been shown for the deep structure of a transformational description by Fillmore, 1966). There are several types of units on this level that are—in certain contexts—realized by the subject or by the object on the phenogrammatical level; it is not yet clear, however, what particular types of units are involved.[8]

If such criteria as those suggested by Fillmore are used, then some facts would indicate that there are more such types, some of them very specific; if we admit that "there is a semantically relevant relation between *the door* and *open* that is the same" in the sentences *The door will open* and *The janitor will open the door* (Fillmore, 1966, p. 4), we shall also find that there is such a relation between *Mary* and *marry* that is the same in the sentences *John married Mary* and *Mary married John*, but probably we shall not find any evidence for regarding *Mary* in the second sentence (or *John* in the first) as a goal (we prefer this term to Fillmore's Ergative, which is quite misleading). Does that mean that a new "actant" should be adopted for such a small group of verbs? On the other hand, there are verbs like *precede*, *coincide* whose inanimate subjects could hardly be classed as instruments or goals, so that the assumption that every actor (Agentive) must be animate appears questionable. Such verbs seem to support the view held by Skalička, 1962 and quoted in Section 2.1.1.

It is well known that English differs from most European languages in respect of those properties of verbal constructions that are discussed by Fillmore; not only the wide use and the distribution of prepositions (cf. Zimmermann, 1967), but also such features as the relatively free rules of passivization (connected with the possibility of a Locative becoming Subject, in the terminology of the quoted studies), or the identity of the verbal forms in cases such as the following belong to the peculiarities of English: *he opens the door with that key; that key will open the door; the door opens.* In many other languages a passive or reflexive form of the verb is more typical for constructions corresponding to the third type. There is a danger that the description of these languages might be influenced unsuitably if it is based on assumptions derived from such features specific to English (similarly as was the case of features of Latin).

For Czech, these questions of verbal constructions have not yet been studied systematically,[9] and it would be premature to attempt to solve them here. Therefore, we use here only the functors corresponding to syntactic relations of actor, goal, (free) modification, predicate nominal, and "separate sentence part" (e.g. a vocative; see Section 3.1), namely R_a, R_g, R_m, R_n and R_v, respectively. The different "morphological meanings", rendered in the description by the so-called suffixes contained (in the form of indices) in the complex symbol corresponding to the dependent member of the given syntagm (see the tentative list of some of them in Section 6.2), characterize the semantically different types of free modification (and of some other relations). We are aware of the unclear status of such units as "instrument" or "interest" treated as such suffixes here; if it proves useful to work with "indirect object", "Benefactive", etc. as with "actants", they can be accounted for in a description of the proposed type by further functors. In a detailed elaboration, it will certainly be necessary to distinguish at least three kinds of expansions —namely, the obligatory, regular, and free expansion; but these are distinctions of the type of relationship, not of expanding categories.[10] These questions will have to be studied in connection with those concerning the relative closeness of syntactic relations (see Section 4.1.2).

In any case, such studies as Fillmore's, if confronted with older writings on similar subjects, show clearly how attempts at an explicit description of language reveal unclear points in our knowledge of language and suggest new ways of solving them.

We assume that the lexical semantemes are of several kinds (i.e., a partition is defined on the set of lexical semantemes). Each of the subsets (elements of the partition) contains elements with like syntactic (distributional) features, differing from those of the elements of all other subsets. These subsets are in a sense parallel to the word classes, but since they are classes of elements of a higher level, they are here termed semantic word classes (SWC). The partition used here (on the basis of preliminary considerations) is very close to that presented by Dokulil (1962, p. 32) as the classification of onomasiological categories (substance, quality, action, circumstance). Thus we distinguish morphemic, syntactic, and semantic word classes (partitions of the sets of stem morphemes, lexical tagmemes, and lexical semantemes, respectively).

It is assumed that sentences as (1) and (2) have at least one meaning in common

(1) *Po Karlově náhlém příjezdu diskuse pokračovala.* (*After Charles' sudden arrival the discussion continued.*)

(2) *Když Karel náhle přijel, diskuse pokračovala.* (*When Charles had suddenly arrived, the discussion continued.*)

It follows that on the tectogrammatical level a single semanteme corresponds to both the words *příjezd* (*arrival*) and *přijel* (*had arrived*), and another to both *náhlý* (*sudden*) and *náhle* (*suddenly*). More generally, among the relations of word-formation, two main types must be distinguished; Kuryłowicz (1936) has called them *dérivation lexicale* and *dérivation syntaxique*. (Of course, not only derivation in the narrower sense, but all types of formation of naming units are concerned.) In cases where two naming units differ only in their syntactic properties (and in that they belong to different syntactic word classes), and not in their lexical meaning, that is, in the case of syntactic derivation, both naming units correspond to the same lexical semanteme.

Certainly, it is very difficult to find appropriate criteria for distinguishing between lexical and syntactic derivation in individual cases. It is necessary to provide for a wide homonymy among verbal nouns, for instance, and various nouns derived from verbs, but differing from them by some feature of their lexical meaning (cf. *his being ill* and *human being*, or *revision* as the name of a process and of its result).

The partition of the set of lexical semantemes as well as that of the set of lexical tagmemes specifies the ranges of individual "variables" used in the notation of our generative description of a language (in rule schemata, cf. Section 4.1.3). It is still an open question whether the lexical semantemes (and tagmemes) should be regarded as elementary or as complex symbols. In some parts of the generative description the complex symbols would be treated as single symbols, while in others they would be decomposed into their elements (among which some would correspond to appurtenance to this or that element of the said partition). In this book, the former of these two possibilities is followed, since we are not concerned here specifically with questions of lexical semantics; however, in further elaboration it will presumably be more appropriate to choose the other, which presupposes a reformulation of the formal properties of the description in this respect.

As at the phenogrammatical level, one can speak of a "tectogrammatical (semantic) word-form", consisting of a lexical semanteme with a certain number of suffixes (and a functor), and of a tectogrammatical (semantic) word.

The complex unit of the tectogrammatical level is the proposition, which can be specified as a well-formed formula of a calculus; the functors of the shape R_i have a position here similar to that of functors with two arguments in the Polish notation for the propositional calculus, but they are written to the right, not to the left of their arguments. A proposition is regarded here as a representation of a sentence on the tectogrammatical level; however, a description of language certainly should account for cases of synonymy between a single sentence and a sequence of several sentences; so that it appears necessary to reckon with cases where a single proposition is realized by a sequence of sentences.[11]

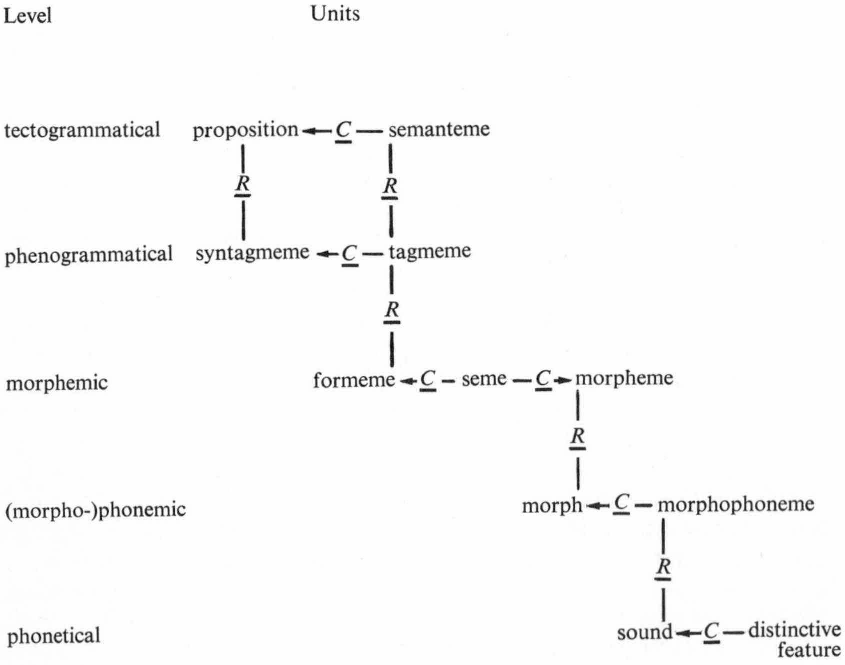

Note. The arrow points to the complex unit.

Figure 4. Main Types of Units.

The overall scheme of levels and main types of units is formulated with relations of type *R* and of type *C*. Certain types of units lack counterparts on some level. A certain asymmetry can be found as regards Figure 4. Further, there are such units as the syllable, the breath unit as a string of syllables, and the rhythm unit as a string of breath units, which show that the relations of type *C* are to a certain degree independent of those of type *R*. This independence of relations of type *C* is, of course, limited: there is a relationship, for instance, between the breath unit and the (morphemic) word-form (they differ in such cases as a prepositional phrase with a single stress), and also the intonation articulation of larger units is connected with the semantic structure of the sentence and other aspects concerning higher levels, especially with functional sentence perspective (Daneš, 1957, Part III). The latter relationship is not accounted for in the proposed description.

2.1.4 REMARKS ON THE SYSTEM OF LEVELS

For each level it is necessary to specify:

(a) the set of elementary units of the level; in a generative system these elements are given in various subsets of rules (mostly in the selection rules of the generative component and, in the case of the system proposed here, in several tables belonging to the transducing components);

(b) certain relations of type *C*, that is, relations between elementary units that constitute complex units (or the corresponding operations[12]); the set of all virtual complex units on any level is given by the set of elementary units of that level and its relations of type *C*;

(c) the subset of the set mentioned in (b) whose elements are the well-formed complex units, that is, units meeting the restrictions that could be formulated directly for the given level, by means of its own "grammar" (cf. Hays, 1964, Section 7, or the tactic patterns of Lamb, 1966b); (the distinction between (b) and (c) is probably not essential; cf. the comments below);

(d) the set of complex units that are not only well formed, but also "actual," that is, which occur in representations of grammatical sentences (point (a) of the assumption from Section 1.3.4 concerns these actual units);

(e) a partition of the set of elementary units, corresponding to the differences in their position as to the relations of type *C* (cf. for instance the above-mentioned partition of tagmemes into lexical tagmemes, suffixes and sentence parts, or into more specific subsets; or the similar partition of semantemes);

(f) a specification of the representation of the sentence on the given level; the representation of the sentence is a complex unit on each of the two highest levels (cf. Section 2.1.3) and need not be specified separately from (c); as to the lower levels, where the representation of the sentence may contain several complex units, a special boundary symbol is presupposed, corresponding to the final intonation contour (possibly together with a certain type of pause).[13]

Some of the points given above correspond more or less precisely to the specification of a level of the language system known from the works of Chomsky (cf. Section 1.3.3). The main difference lies in the fact that Chomsky mentions the specification of elementary symbols only, not that of the complex ones, while we reckon with complex units and relations of type *C*. It follows that no *L*-markers are needed in the system proposed here; the structural description of a sentence can be defined as a sequence of its representations on individual levels, that is, a sequence of the form $(r_1, r_2, \ldots, r_n)$, where r_i is the representation of the sentence on the *i*-th level for $1 \leqq i \leqq n$, the levels being numbered from the tectogrammatical to the phonetic, and *n* is the number of levels.

Point (e) has no direct counterpart in Chomsky's treatment; it is not necessary there, since only a concatenation of elementary units of the given level is used. The distinction between virtual and well-formed units can perhaps be abandoned, if the transducing components of the generative system are formulated accordingly (so that only well-formed complex units can be present in the strings of the input and output languages of those components; cf. Section 2.2.5).

Let us assume that the elementary units of individual levels are given. Those of the phonetic level are the distinctive features, specified either articulatorily, acoustically, or, as the case may be, by more complex means (cf. Vachek, in press, for Czech); in addition there are units such as stress and various intonational contours (Daneš, 1957). In Czech, stress does not belong to the distinctive features, but – along with intonational contours – to the so-called prosodic features. The typical elementary unit of the morphophonemic level is the morphophoneme[14]; certain boundary symbols are also needed, in particular the juncture between morphs, the word boundary, and symbols realized by intonational contours. On the morphemic level it is also necessary—alongside the semes, which are the basic type of elementary units—to reckon with certain boundary symbols. On the higher levels, besides the elementary units shown in Figure 4, similar devices should perhaps be used (cf. Section 4.2.1).

As to points (b) to (e), on the phonetic level the distinctive features are divided into such subsets as voiced–voiceless, short–long, etc. A virtual sound can be specified as a combination of distinctive features from these subsets (which are mutually disjoint; cf. Section 2.1.2). The set of well-formed sounds is, however, only a proper subset of the set of virtual sounds (in English as well as in Czech, for instance, the feature voiceless cannot be combined with that of nasality). The set of all actual sounds is a subset of the set of well-formed sounds of the given language, although in most cases, perhaps, the two latter sets are identical.

At the morphophonemic level, the morphophonemes are divided into several subsets according to their distributional features. The complex unit morph (the virtual one) can be characterized informally as a string of morphophonemes. The set of well-formed morphs can be specified by certain rules restricting the possibilities of concatenating the morphophonemes belonging to distributional subsets. The set of actual morphs cannot be specified simply as the set of strings realizing morphemes, because of cases of horizontal asymmetry; this difficulty, as is well known, can be overcome in a generative description, where cases of horizontal asymmetry play the role of individual deviations, but not that of counterexamples.

The elementary units of the morphemic level are the semes. The relevant subsets of lexical semes are morphemic word classes,[15] and those of grammatical semes are grammatical categories (cases, numbers, genders, persons, tenses, moods, etc.).

The relations of type *C* on this level are similar to those on the phonetic level (cf. Section 2.1.2).

The complex units of the two levels of sentence structure were set forth in Section 2.1.3.

The relation of realization is a many-to-many relation, on account of what is called asymmetrical dualism. So there exist sentences that are homonymous or synonymous at different levels. Moreover, it is possible, for example, that a single proposition has two different representations on the phenogrammatical level or on that of morphemics, and both are realized by the same phonetic means – cf. English *The jury came in* (corresponding either to *The jury is coming in* or to *The jury are coming in*) – so that there is synonymy above homonymy. In other cases there is homonymy above synonymy (e.g. *They are flying planes* – in an idiolect where the morph *ing* can be realized by two synonymous means, *iŋ* and *in*). The former of these examples is a sentence that is assigned two structural descriptions, but can hardly be conceived to have two distinct senses. This is provided for, in the proposed system, by the fact that the two structural descriptions contain only a single proposition. Moreover, it would be difficult here to speak of paraphrases, since only a single sentence is concerned. Two pairs of terms should then be distinguished, namely homonymy and synonymy (relativized to the individual levels, or, more precisely, to pairs of adjacent levels), and ambiguity and paraphrase (where a sentence corresponds to two or more propositions and *vice versa*).

2.1.5 CONFRONTATION WITH LAMB'S STRATIFICATIONAL LINGUISTICS

As can be seen from the preceding sections (and as has been stated in Section 1.2), our general standpoint concerning the relationships among levels as well as those among their units has much in common with that of S. M. Lamb's stratificational linguistics (cf. especially Lamb, 1966b). This agreement in the general standpoint does not of course exclude divergences in the elaboration of the description. It appears useful to give here at least a short account of these divergences, which neither concern terminology alone, nor are merely imposed by the peculiarities of the languages on which our description is primarily based.

First we make some remarks concerning the choice of levels and units.

From what has been said in Section 2.1.2 about Hockett's (1961) schemes (Figures 1 and 2), it can be seen that we have found it useful to treat separately the two relations called *R* and *C* by Hockett; we have arrived at the scheme (for the lower levels) illustrated in Figure 3. Lamb's treatment differs from ours in that he inserts a new unit (his *morpheme*) between Hockett's *morpheme* (Lamb's *lexon*) and the *morph* (a string of phonemes); see Figure 5. But, in

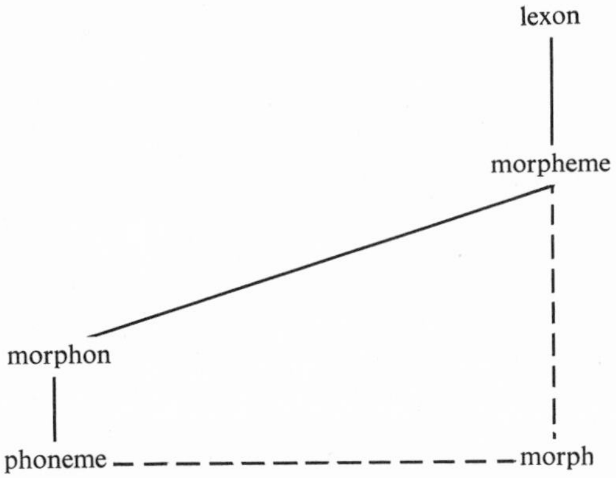

Figure 5. Morphons and Morphemes.

Lamb's scheme, the relationship between morphon and morpheme includes not only Hockett's relation *C* (i.e., Lamb's downward ANDS), but also his relation *R* (Lamb's realization; cf. his portmanteau realization and neutralization in Lamb, 1966b, Figure 6). With this treatment, the fact that individual elementary units (the morphons, in this case) occur as elements of distinct complex units is handled in the same way as homonymy (neutralization) in other cases. (Lamb's upward ORS at the bottom of his sign pattern characterize the elements of complex units, whereas the same graphic means at the bottom of other patterns corresponds to neutralization, if we understand the diagrams correctly.) This means that the presence of the morphon *t* in *sit*, *take*, etc. is regarded as a function of this morphon (in the same way as the semon *plural* is a function of the lexeme *-s*, or the lexon *-s* is a function of the morpheme *-s*).[16]

As to the higher levels, the question remains whether their structure resembles that of the morphemic level closely enough that the corresponding patterns of distinct levels can be characterized by the same scheme, especially if the representation of a sentence on the sememic level has the form of a network (cf. Lamb, 1964a, b; Hockett, 1966, pp. 272ff), whereas on the lower levels, the sentence is represented by a string or a sequence of units.

It is true that the scheme of units in the type of description we propose, as illustrated in Figure 4, is not so balanced and regularly shaped as that of Lamb (cf. Figure 8 in Lamb, 1966b). But this need not be considered a shortcoming of our approach; if the graphic notation of Lamb's patterns (Figure 6 and others in Lamb, 1966b) is considered, the question arises whether the straightforwardness of the general scheme of units (Figure 8) has not been gained only at the price of a loss of simplicity and regularity of the stratificational description itself. It is not clear, namely, what regularities and restrictions govern the distribution of the ANDS and ORS in Lamb's four types of patterns. It remains uncertain whether there is a maximum number of nodes that can be passed through by an impulse moving downward (or upward) inside a single pattern (and, further, what restrictions are laid upon the arrangement of nodes of different types in a certain pattern). It is not easy to understand, for instance, why $well_1$ (the noun) and $well_2$ (the adverb) are regarded as two distinct morphemes (cf. Lamb, 1966b, p. 58), and not as two lexons realized by a single morpheme. If the latter solution were chosen, it would be possible—if we understand Lamb's exposition correctly—to do without the neutralizations in the knot patterns, where they appear only occasionally. Perhaps Lamb prefers the former solution in order to make it possible to account for the distinct syntactic distribution of the two units in question by his morphotactics; but we may ask why this distribution should be accounted for just by the morphotactics and not, for instance, by the lexotactics. Only an elaboration based on comprehensive empirical work can decide questions of this kind.

Instead of working with a fully balanced general scheme of levels and units, and accepting these difficulties in stating the formal properties of the description itself, we prefer to have a less symmetric scheme of levels and units allowing the description itself to be formulated in a relatively simple way. We have found, for instance, that the structure of some pairs of levels can be conceived as parallel to a relatively high degree (cf. for instance the phonetic and morphemic levels, or perhaps the two levels of sentence structure), but that it is not so closely related to the structure of other levels. It is not surprising that the higher levels are in some respects structured like certain logical calculi, but the phonetic level (as well as the phonemic and morphemic) is certainly of a different kind. As has been stated above, these differences should be shown in some way by the general scheme of levels and units. In any case, we regard such schemes (as that given in Figure 4) solely as a means for a better orientation in the informal account of the description, whereas the main theoretical aim to be achieved is an explicit formulation of a generative system corresponding to the main principles cited in Section 1.1.

Most of the differences we have found between Lamb's stratificational linguistics and the approach proposed here concern the treatment of technical questions. On the other hand, the underlying ideas are to a great extent common or parallel: the relation between content and expression (in Hjelmslev's terminology) is articulated into several relations between neighboring strata or levels. This is connected with the general shape of the system, where a level corresponding in some way to the sense of sentences is specified by a generative component (with recursive properties), whereas the representations of sentences on the other levels are gained by some kind of transducer.

This common view of the hierarchy of levels, of course, helps explain our common attitude toward the development of transformational theory dating from 1964–1965.[17]

Besides these common theoretical standpoints there are also various more or less empirically conditioned agreements, such as for example the use of dependency syntax.

The differences mentioned above are mostly of such a nature that they can be reduced in the course of further empirical study, which will bring evidence for some of the proposed solutions—or for others—and which will make a more systematic confrontation of the two approaches possible.

2.1.6 CRITERIA FOR THE DECOMPOSITION OF THE DESCRIPTION INTO LEVELS

Our formulation of the levels is consciously based—to a certain extent—on traditional notions (cf. Section 2.1.1), but for further elaboration general criteria should be found, enabling the linguist to say whether it is appropriate to work with such and such level (e.g. another level should be inserted between two of the levels he has already established). Economy of description should serve as the main criterion. There are some indications as to circumstances under which such an insertion of a new level can be considered useful from this point of view. One of them was expressed in the eighth axiom of the system presented in Nebeský and Sgall (1962). We reproduce this axiom here as a necessary condition laid upon the distribution of units into levels.

If the units of two levels standing in the relation of realization are called form and function (functions are realized by forms), the condition in question can be formulated by means of four single statements:

(a) x and y are two distinct forms, v and z are two distinct functions;

(b) x realizes v, x realizes z, y realizes v, y realizes z;

(c) the context (including situation) in which x realizes v but not z is identical with the context (including situation) in which y realizes v but not z (by context a relevant feature of context or a set of individual contexts specified by such a feature is understood);

(d) v is realized by x but not by y exactly in the same context in which z is realized by x but not by y.

Then the condition may be stated as follows: If (a), (b), and (c) hold, then (d) does not hold. This condition will be called the condition of distinct contexts. If a tentative description does not fulfill this condition, then it may be useful to consider whether a new level should be inserted.

Let *go* (as a morph) be taken for x, *went* for y, one of the meanings of the verb (e.g. that of German *gehen*) for v and another of its meanings (e.g. that of German *fahren*) for z. It is evident that (a) and (b) hold. The same is true with (c) since *go* realizes the meaning of *gehen* in contexts characterized by the same relevant feature as the contexts in which the morph *went* realizes this meaning. (It would not, however, be an easy task to define such a relevant feature.) If the condition of distinct contexts were satisfied, then (d) could not hold; but we see that the relevant feature determining the use of the morphs *go* and *went* in the meaning of *gehen* is the same as that determining the use of these morphs in the meaning of *fahren*. In both cases the corresponding morph is chosen according to the seme of tense with which the given meaning is connected. This distribution of units contradicts our condition, and this contradiction can be avoided by interpolating a new level between the two existing ones (*viz.* the morphemic level in our example, with the lexical seme of the cited verb).

In other words, the distinction between the morphs *go* and *went* is not relevant for the relationship of such units as the two meanings mentioned and both morphs can be regarded as mere variants of a single unit realizing those meanings. It is a well-known fact that in the development of linguistics similar considerations led to the insertion of a new level, namely the phonemic, between phonetics and morphemics. It might be useful to apply this criterion to other levels as well, especially to the higher levels, where the problems are much more complex.

We have already said that we want to work with a level that would correspond to the semantic structure of the sentence as it has been understood by some members of the Prague School. The question remains, then, whether two levels of sentence structure should be distinguished. If the criterion of distinct contexts is to be used, such cases as the following have to be considered:

On the tectogrammatical level of Czech, units such as actor and goal may be taken for the functions *v* and *z*, respectively, and the genitive case and possessive adjective for the forms *x* and *y*. (There exist other forms, too, but this is not relevant for our consideration.) For example, given two Czech phrases, *Karlův odchod* (*Charles' departure*), and *odchod našeho Karla* (*the departure of our Charles*), in each of them the function *v* is present, while in *Karlovo překvapení* (*Charles' surprise* or *Charles' surprising someone*)[18] as well as in *překvapení našeho Karla* (*the surprise of our Charles* or *the surprise of someone by our Charles*) both the functions *v* and *z* can be realized. (Sometimes, in Czech, this homonymy can be solved on the basis of other features of the context, for example when the word *překvapení* (*surprise*) is modified by the instrumental case of a noun, functioning as the actor.) If the relevant feature of the context is supposed to be the same both for the possessive adjective and for the genitive case (i.e., the statement (c) holds), then the condition of distinct contexts will not be fulfilled, since (a), (b) and (d) evidently hold for the given example. On the other hand, the condition will be met if a new unit (that from the phenogrammatical level, namely the attributive) is inserted between the two levels in question.

When lexical units are involved, the same process can be applied, should the necessity of two levels above the morphemic level be examined. We assume that a more detailed examination would confirm the demand for the distinction of the two levels; it is not difficult to find two (semi-)synonymous words that have several meanings in common without the condition of distinct contexts being fulfilled; cf. for instance the pair *to begin—to start* cited in Section 2.1.2, or pairs such as *require-demand* in English and *brzo—brzy* (*soon*), *stále—pořád* (*all the time*) in Czech.

The application of the condition of distinct contexts confirms the assumption that in a description of language at least two levels higher than the morphemic level must be incorporated. But it will be necessary to examine the question whether fulfillment of our condition always implies greater economy of the system.

We have tried (Sgall, 1967a), to choose an illustrative example, which has shown that there are good reasons for taking the condition of distinct contexts into consideration even if we cannot claim to have shown that it will lead to simpler description in all cases. To solve the problem it would be necessary to study it in a quite general manner by appropriate formal means.

2.2 FORMAL DEVICES USED

2.2.1 PRELIMINARY CONSIDERATIONS

Our investigation of the mathematical means to be employed in the description started from the following considerations: The formal device(s) used should allow for a confrontation with systems defined in automata theory and in the theory of grammar. The weak generative power of the means chosen should be less than that of a universal Turing machine (i.e., not equivalent to it, and not even weakly equivalent in the sense of Evey, 1963); we desired to work with means specific enough to be interesting (cf. Chomsky, 1961, Note 27). As far as is known (according to the literature now available), such a device cannot be stronger than a pushdown transducer or a context-free phrase-structure grammar. Weaker devices could hardly be used as a means for describing levels where other than purely local context criteria are relevant, since none of these devices—as far as we know— makes it possible to account for qualitative relationships between substrings separated by an indefinite number of intervening symbols.

Having the above considerations in mind, we were to choose between the following two possibilities (cf. the two alternative wordings of point (d) in the assumption of Section 1.3.4): First, the description as a whole could be weakly equivalent (equivalent in the sense of Chomsky, 1959) with a context-free phrase-structure grammar, that is, its terminal language would be context-free. This possibility—with respect to transformational grammars—was not denied in the first years of Chomsky's work on the theory of grammar. Moreover, as is sometimes pointed out, it can hardly be accidental that so many scholars using rather different approaches to investigate the structure of natural languages have formulated systems of this kind. Nevertheless, there are several indications that the weak generative power of these systems is inadequate (cf. Bar-Hillel, 1964, pp. 193f). Postal (1964, pp. 75ff) argues most strongly to this effect. It would be of great importance to check these arguments as thoroughly as possible; it is difficult to find out, for instance, whether the indefinitely long noun stems in Mohawk could be accounted for in some other way; the English construction with *respectively* probably originated in technical usage (and even today it is confined to some stylistic strata only, and is not found in everyday colloquial speech), so that it need not be considered characteristic of the natural language as such; these arguments apply also to the properties of numerals mentioned sometimes in this connection. Of course, the objections of Postal and others are not invalidated by such remarks; we only want to show that it would be premature to insist unreservedly that context-free languages are not adequate as models of natural languages.

The other possibility is to formulate a description the terminal language of which is not necessarily context-free (so that the objections mentioned could be met), but in which each of the component devices is weakly equivalent to a context-free phrase-structure grammar (see Section 2.2.5). If the description of language were characterized in general as a finite sequence of such components (where the i-th component translates any string of the output language of the $(i-1)$-th component into some string of the input language of the $(i+1)$-th component, for $1 \leqslant i \leqslant n$, n being the number of components), then Chomsky's requirement that the description have a specific character would be satisfied,[19] even if the output language were not necessarily context-free. In a sense, such specification is parallel to that of transformational grammar. To meet the requirement of Putnam (1961), the description has to satisfy conditions guaranteeing that a recognition routine for it exists (cf. Section 2.2.5).

2.2.2 GRAPHS AND AUTOMATA

In the linguistic tradition mentioned in Section 2.1.1, a means is often used in modelling the structure of a sentence that is suited to a relatively straightforward formal definition. These means, the well-known diagrams of Tesnière (1959), or those of Šmilauer (1947, 1957) and others, can easily be reformulated as special types of graphs (cf. e.g. Harper and Hays, 1960; Lecerf, 1960; Hays, 1961). One possible definition of this type of graphs is as follows:

A *labelled projective rooted tree* is defined as a quintuple (M, V, T, R, W) where

M is an abstract finite set (interpreted as the set of nodes);

V is a finite set of symbols (interpreted as the vocabulary of the level);

T is a mapping of M into V;

R is a binary relation on M such that the graph (M, R) is a directed rooted tree, that is a connected graph fulfilling the following conditions: there is exactly one m_r in M such that $R(m_r, m_j)$ holds for no m_j (this node is called the root of the tree); for every m_i in M which is distinct from m_r there is exactly one m_j such that $R(m_i, m_j)$; $R(m_i, m_j)$ can be read as "m_i depends on m_j" and interpreted as the relation of ("immediate") dependency;

W is a relation of strict ordering on M that meets the condition of projectivity, that is, for any m_i, m_j, m_k in M, if $R(m_i, m_j)$ and either $W(m_i, m_k)$ and $W(m_k, m_j)$, or $W(m_j, m_k)$ and $W(m_k, m_i)$, then $\bar{R}(m_k, m_j)$ where $\bar{R}$ is the transitive closure of R; $W(m_i, m_j)$ is read as "m_i precedes m_j" and interpreted as the relative position of the two units as to the word order.

Trees of this type (with an equivalent definition) have been investigated by Pospíšil (1966); some possibilities of their use in linguistics are dealt with in Sgall (1967c); on the notion of projectivity see Marcus (1965) and the literature quoted there.

Such trees (and other, more or less closely related types of dependency trees) can be used as formal counterparts of the diagrams mentioned above, with some slight modifications (e.g. Tesnière's diagrams have to be modified so as to model the word order, too; Šmilauer's way of representing the sentence needs to be altered in that the relation of subject to predicate is to be taken in the terms of graphs as a kind of dependency, not as a special type of relation). In classical linguistics the above-mentioned diagrams have been used for the description of the syntactic (grammatical) structure of the sentence, that is, they correspond to our phenogrammatical level.[20] But—as far as one can judge from a few points concerning the level of the semantic structure of the sentence,[21] which has not yet been studied in a systematic way—it would be possible even in the description of this higher level to work (at least in a preliminary way) with a dependency relation possessing the said formal properties. In this case the tectogrammatical, as well as the phenogrammatical structure of a sentence could be represented by a labelled projective rooted tree.

But then a procedure would be necessary that transduces trees into trees; to put it more precisely, an effective procedure needs to be formulated which specifies a general mapping of a certain subset of labelled projective rooted trees (specified by means of some generating device; see e.g. Sgall, 1967c) into the set of such trees. Since such a procedure—or device—has to operate with graphs (or bidimensional diagrams) instead of strings as the elements of its input and output languages, it is also necessary to specify its relationship to the known types of grammars and automata (for instance to find the basis for the confrontation of sets of graphs with sets of strings); otherwise no connection can be found between the proposed type of description and the known theorems of automata theory.

These questions have so far been elucidated only in part. It has been shown (cf. Pospíšil, 1966) that there exists a one-to-one mapping of the set of all projective trees whose nodes are labelled with symbols of a certain alphabet V (a finite set of symbols containing neither the symbol ϕ nor the symbol ϕ') onto a set of strings called L_v and defined with the aid of another set of strings (denoted L) as follows:

(i) $V \subset L \subset L_V$
(ii) if $x,y \in L_V$, then $\phi' xy \in L_V$
(iii) if $x \in L_V$, $y \in L$, then $\phi xy \in L$
(iv) no other element is an element either of L_v or of L.

It is possible to work with L_v as the input (output) language of some of the components of the description proposed here (cf. Sgall, 1966; 1967a); the input languages of the automata $\mathbf{T}_{2n}$ defined in Chapter 5 below would contain L_v only as a proper subset, but the strings belonging to them and not to L_v cannot occur in the generation of a sentence (nor in its structural description) since this is excluded by the form of the grammar and of the first automaton. We can therefore say that there is a certain correspondence between dependency graphs and the languages of our automata.

But before this correspondence has been characterized more fully (and before a procedure has been formulated that transduces such graphs and is in some sense equivalent to one of the transducing components of our description), there is no possibility of an explicit confrontation between systems using graphs and those using grammars and automata. Therefore in this book, too, we prefer to work with a formalism including devices that have been thoroughly studied mathematically, even if the linguistic evaluation of such a description meets with some difficulties (cf. Section 2.2.4).

As to the distinction between grammars and automata, we do not consider it to be so important as it might appear at first sight, since a grammar can be reformulated as a transducer (having—in most cases—only one single string in its input language); it seems appropriate to give to the generative component the form of a grammar, while the transducing ("interpretive") components are formulated as transducers. We assume that, in this case, the latter components can have a more transparent relationship to their linguistic evaluation than such devices as Hockett's (1966) grammars with input sets consisting of sets of rules.

2.2.3 THE GENERATIVE COMPONENT

The first component of our sequence of devices, in which the recursive properties of the system are concentrated,[22] should account for the phrase structure of a proposition as well as for its dependency structure. According to Chomsky (1965, pp. 68ff), the information concerning the dependency structure could be extracted directly from the rules (or P-markers) of a context-free phrase-structure grammar (and from a set of definitions that need not be included in the description, since they form a part of the general linguistic theory). But this presupposes that there is the same kind of dependence (of "syntactic function", in Chomsky's terminology) whenever a phrase of a certain type is a constituent of another phrase (e.g. *NP* as a constituent of a *VP* is necessarily an object of this *VP*); and it is not certain if this can be taken for granted. Furthermore, it would not be simple to refer to this kind of information when using further (transducing) rules;[23] cf. now also the difficulties pointed out by Fillmore (1966).

On the other hand, some of the scholars working with dependency grammars try to characterize even the phrase structure (or, better, the closeness of relation) by this means; they distinguish, for instance, an adverbial phrase depending on the verb as such from a phrase (otherwise syntactically equivalent) depending on the sentence (or verbal phrase, etc.) as a whole, by using a distinct kind of dependence (a special rule, etc.) for each of them.[24] But this way of handling the phrase-structure distinction seems to have its drawbacks, too. The distinction mentioned is, at least in some cases, graded, so that it is not possible to describe it adequately by a certain number of different kinds of dependence (cf. phrases such as *a broken wooden dining table*, as characterized by Šmilauer, 1947, § 5.97). It is a distinction in the closeness of dependence, not in its kind, so that it is more properly accounted for by some such means as parenthesizing, than by a qualitative characterization. In many cases these drawbacks can be avoided by characterizing the given distinctions in terms of word order or by similar means, but it is not certain whether all cases can be treated thus (even if the order of elements in the deep structure or on the tectogrammatical level is distinguished from the "surface" order of word forms).

In Czech, the difference between (1) and (2), when pronounced with neutral intonation, is semantically relevant (and must be respected in a good translation):

(1) *Přišel kvůli Karlovi včera.*
(*It was yesterday that he came for Charles' sake.*)

(2) *Přišel včera kvůli Karlovi.*
(*It was for Charles' sake that he came yesterday.*)

The closeness of the syntactic relation in the Czech examples is rendered by the word order; but it is not necessarily rendered by this means. The speaker and the hearer may be aware of such a distinction in the closeness of the relation of the two adverbials to the verb even in (3), where it is not rendered by their position. (It can be rendered by intonation, or it can be evident from the fact that the sentence is used as an answer to this or that question, etc.)

(3) *Včera přišel kvůli Karlovi.*
(*Yesterday he came for Charles' sake.*)

Therefore in the specification of the tectogrammatical level by the first component of our generative description, we use besides the relation of dependence (described by the functors), also means corresponding to those used in a phrase-structure grammar. Thus our first component has the form of a context-free phrase-structure grammar,[25] and not that of a dependency grammar (as defined formally by Gaifman, 1961 or Hays, 1961, 1964, and further analyzed by Novák, 1966b). But we are aware of the fact that even so we are not able to account fully for the closeness of the syntactic relation and that it is partly confused with other phenomena (cf. Note 1 to Chapter 2 and Section 4.1.2).

While a formal presentation of the devices is reserved for Chapter 5, we would like to mention here that the generative component is of a special type, that is, not only does it meet the conditions laid down on a context-free grammar, but its expansion rules have a special form, connected with the types of elementary units of the tectogrammatical level, which is identical to the terminal language generated by this component. In Section 2.1.3. we have characterized three types of these units, namely the lexical semantemes, the suffixes, and the functors. For an explicit treatment of the generative component it seems appropriate to combine a lexical semanteme (as well as a corresponding non-terminal symbol from which the lexical semanteme can be derived) with its suffixes into a single complex symbol. In our formalism this complex symbol is treated as elementary, and consequently there is a gap between the formal status of the grammar and its interpretation. We use rule schemata and conventions so that the notation shows where a lack of generalization remains; it is an open question whether these notational devices can be incorporated into the general linguistic theory (cf. Chomsky, 1965, § 7 of Part 1), or whether a new definition of the grammar is to be preferred, enabling it to include complex symbols as such (i.e., under certain conditions more than one elementary symbol could be rewritten according to one rule, cf. Section 4.1.3). It can be shown that even such a grammar would be weakly equivalent to a context-free phrase-structure grammar.

The expansion rules of the generative component have the form $A \rightarrow B\ C\ R$, where A, B, C are (complex) symbols and R is a functor (with or without a prime). In a derived string the placement of the functors points to the relative closeness of the individual syntagms. Moreover, B is interpreted as the dependent and C as the governing symbol (i.e., the modifier and the head of the syntagm, respectively, are derived from them), if R is a functor without a prime, while a functor with a prime is used in the event that the left-hand symbol is the governor.

As we have already mentioned, no P-marker is used as a part of the structural description of a sentence in the proposed system. Only the terminal string (i.e., the representation of the sentence on the tectogrammatical level, the proposition) is a part of the structural description (cf. Section 2.1.4).

A formal definition of a grammar that can serve as the generative component is given in Section 5.2; a preliminary fragment (for the Czech language) in Section 6.2; some linguistic questions are commented in Chapter 3.

2.2.4 THE TRANSDUCTIVE COMPONENTS

The remaining components of the proposed description are transductive, that is, without recursive properties. Each of them translates the representation of a sentence from one level to the next lower one. We work here with pushdown transducers, for reasons sketched in Sections 2.2.1 and 2.2.2. But it is not possible, in general, to translate the representation of a sentence from the tectogrammatical level to the phenogrammatical (nor from this level to the morphemic) using one single transducer of that type. Therefore for each of the first two components we use a sequence of two pushdown transducers of a special type (cf. Section 5.2 for formal definitions, 6.3 to 6.5 for an illustrative application to the Czech language, and 3.4 for informal comments). Each of the four transducers reads the input tape from right to left and prints the output from left to right.

The role of the first of the two transducers in such a sequence is, primarily, to change the order of symbols so that it corresponds to the order of the type "*regens post rectum*" (where every symbol stands to the right of all symbols depending on it); when needed, the transducer changes any symbol in accordance with symbols depending on it (some examples are given in Section 6.4).[26] The second member of the pair of transducers restores the original word order (or makes some changes in it, when necessary—in particular, the fourth transducer changes the position of members of constructions in which the word order on the morphemic level is not in accordance with the condition of projectivity, and places prepositions and conjunctions at the beginning of noun or verb phrases).[27] Furthermore, this second member changes the symbols of the higher level into the corresponding ones of the next lower level (choosing the realizing symbol in accordance with the properties of the governing symbol; cf. Section 6.4).

In the Czech version (Sgall, 1967a) another variant of the transducing components has been used: there the second transducer leaves the symbols in the order "*regens post rectum*", the third transducer changes them to those of the morphemic level, and only the fourth transducer changes the order of symbols so as to yield the actual word order. In that variant $n+2$ transducers are necessary for n pairs of adjacent levels and only two of them are designed primarily to change the order of symbols. On the other hand, the variant used in the present book has an advantage in that the n pairs of transducers are parallel in structure. Since for $n=2$ four automata are needed for both variants, we have chosen the latter possibility here so that a confrontation is possible (or, what is even more important, it is now possible to utilize both versions in formulating the transducing components in terms of the theory of graphs; cf. Section 2.2.2).

The main principle in the functioning of these transducers is to let the governing symbol (or some symbol denoting its syntactic properties) "wait" in the pushdown store until all symbols depending on it are printed in the output. Thus, for instance, a sentence whose structure (on the tectogrammatical as well as the phenogrammatical levels) corresponds to the tree of Figure 6 would have, in the output languages of the respective transducers, the representations shown below, where (0) is the proposition,[28] as generated by the generative component; of course, only the strings marked by even numbers would form a part of the structural description of the sentence, since they alone are representations of the sentence on certain levels of the system (cf. Theorem 2 of Chapter 5, ensuring that a sequence of representations of a sentence on all levels determines uniquely the whole process of transduction).

Distinctions between symbols of different levels are omitted in this example, and indices on the functors are chosen in such a way as to refer to the governed symbol of the corresponding syntagm.

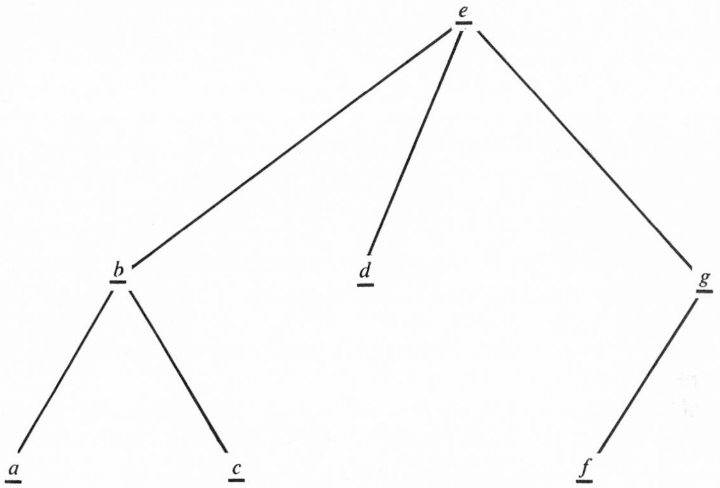

Figure 6. Diagram of a Dependency Tree.

(0) $a\, b\, R_a\, c\, R'_c\, d\, e\, R_d\, f\, g\, R_f\, R'_g\, R_b$
(1) $\phi\, \phi\, f\, g'\, \phi\, d\, \phi\, \phi\, c'\, \phi\, a\, b\, e$
(2) $a\, b\, \phi\, c\, \phi'\, d\, e\, \phi\, \phi\, f\, g\, \phi\, \phi'$
(3) = (1)
(4) = (2)

It is necessary not only to describe the particular strings as representations of the same sentence, but also to account for the fact that a certain morph realizes a certain morpheme, or that a certain formeme realizes a certain tagmeme, etc., in the case given (cf. Note 12 to Chapter 1, for the term "to realize"; in this case, however, the mentioned term is used for a relationship holding between certain parts of different representations of a particular sentence, not for the general relation holding between units of adjacent levels). A definition is needed (not inside an individual grammar, but in the linguistic theory) that would specify an image of a symbol under the operation of transducing sentences from one level to another. We do not attempt to give the definition here, since this needs formal elaboration of an empirically more complete model than we can present by now. For most cases some mathematically trivial (even if somewhat troublesome) means would do, based, for instance, on sequences of rules such as 2, 4, 5, 4, 7, 9 of $\mathbf{T}_{2k-1}$ in Section 5.2, where the symbol printed at the output according to the last rule can be defined as the image of the symbol read at the input according to the first; the mapping $\mathbf{t}_i$ for $1 \leqslant i \leqslant 4$ (see the corresponding tables in Section 6.4) are relevant for this definition; of course, two subsequent transducers must be taken into account, so that a form realizing a function is an image of its image.

But the major obstacle is connected with cases of "horizontal asymmetry"; it is necessary to investigate first, what—in an explicit description—should be the correlate of such statements as "the relative time is realized by verbal tense in clauses of type 1, but by verbal aspect in clauses of type 2" (cf. Panevová, in prep.). In similar cases (e.g. in the case of auxiliary verbs) even the transformational type of structural description of a sentence does not give a direct specification of such interrelation between units of surface and of deep structures. Of course, in both types of description this relationship can be traced back through the whole treatment of the sentence, which is determined uniquely by its structural description: one can go to the elementary transformations, or, in our description, to the individual rules of the transducers used, and find out what unit is a direct or indirect successor of a certain unit of the preceding level.

The changes of the order of symbols exemplified here have only in part a direct linguistic interpretation, but they are necessary if the representation of a sentence on each level is to be a linear formula.

Devices translating the representations of sentences from the morphemic level to the lower levels are not studied here. We assume that they can have the form of devices weakly equivalent (in Chomsky's sense) to finite transducers.

2.2.5 REMARKS ON GENERATIVE POWER

As to the weak generative power of the description as a whole, there are two possibilities: (1) The terminal language of the generative component is identical with the input language of the first transducer, and the output language of any transducer is identical with the input language of its successor in the sequence of transducing devices, down to the last (to the phonetic level), so that the terminal language of the whole description is context-free (cf. the stronger form of the assumption formulated in Section 1.3.4, and the well-known theorems of Chomsky and of Evey stating that an output language of a pushdown transducer is context-free). In this book we do not attempt to formulate the input and output languages of the transducers in such a way as to meet this requirement of identity. (2) There is, at some point(s) in the sequence of devices, only a relation of inclusion instead of identity of the languages (e.g. the terminal language of the generative component is only a proper subset of the input language of the first transducer); in this case the output language of the whole description is not necessarily context-free, since (leaving aside the components transducing sentences from morphemic to phonetic level) it is only a proper subset of the context-free language of the last pushdown transducer.

This second possibility (cf. the weaker formulation of the assumption from Section 1.3.4 and further, Section 2.2.1) is elaborated here, i.e., the individual devices are characterized as components of a single system in that they meet the condition

$$L_G \subset {}^iL_0,\ {}^oL_j \subset {}^iL_{j+1},\ 0 \leqslant j \leqslant 3$$

where ${}^oL_j$ (${}^iL_j$) denotes the output (input) language of the j-th transducer, and L_G the terminal language of the generative component. This condition is provided for by Theorem 1 of Chapter 5.

In this case, a system of the proposed type can be formulated to generate, for instance, the set of all strings of the form $\mathbf{x}\, a\, \mathbf{x}$, where $\mathbf{x}$ is a string over an alphabet not containing a: it is possible to formulate a generative component defining the set of all strings of the form $\mathbf{x}\, a\, \bar{\mathbf{x}}$ (where $\bar{\mathbf{x}}$ is the reflection of $\mathbf{x}$), which is a context-free language, and the transductive part of the system merely reverses the order of symbols in the right part of every string (in the part to the right of the symbol a), which can be done trivially by a pushdown transducer. If our interpretation is correct, it is possible to account in this way for the features of natural languages for which Postal and others claim context-free languages are inadequate, and yet to have a description whose formal properties are specific enough (cf. Section 2.2.1), since—among other properties—the weak generative power of each of its components is limited to that of a context-free phrase-structure grammar.

Another question is, whether in this case the input and output languages of the individual components can serve to specify the syntactic structure of the corresponding levels (cf. Hockett, 1966, p. 229). If some of the distinctions necessary for the formulation of selection restrictions in the generative component were disregarded in the rules of the first transducing component (i.e., the first two members of the sequence of pushdown transducers) then strings excluded by the former component would not be excluded by the latter. Thus, for instance, if a string such as *golf plays John* should be excluded as having no representation on the tectogrammatical level of English,[29] the rules of the first pair of transducers can still be formulated without the distinction of animate and inanimate nouns, so that the input language of the first transducer contains a string that is transduced later as *golf plays John* (but no string transduced e.g. as *with plays the*). Similarly for the other components; for instance a string such as *blik*, but not *ftik*, would be accepted by the transducer mapping morphophonemic strings into phonetic ones, etc.

In this way, the transducing components could play the role of "tactics" in Lamb's stratificational description and contribute to achieving a higher level of adequacy (cf. Chomsky, 1962a, 1965). Of course, their formulation presupposes the elucidation of many unclear empirical questions, and in Chapter 5 we do not attempt to formulate them in this way, but give them a far less specific form, which can serve only as an illustration of possibility (2).

Questions of strong generative power, which are more important linguistically, have not yet been formulated properly from the mathematical standpoint. It is, therefore, not possible to treat them so explicitly as questions of weak generative power. Nevertheless, there are some formulations in the writings of Chomsky and others enabling a general confrontation to be made of transformational and other descriptions in this respect.

One point concerns the distinction between transformational and "taxonomic" grammars (Chomsky, 1962a, § 1.1); one of the relevant properties of transformational grammars is formulated as the possibility that "the symbols and structures that are manipulated, rewritten, and transformed as a sentence is generated may bear no very direct relation to any of its concrete subparts" (*loc. cit.*), so that this type of grammar is not so atomistic as the taxonomic model, where each of the rewritten symbols stands for a category to which some subpart of the sentence belongs. This property of the transformational description is connected with the distinction between deep structure and surface structure, since the symbols corresponding to items of deep structure can be characterized as not related directly to any subpart of the sentence. Moreover, in view of this distinction, it is possible with a transformational description to characterize a subpart of a sentence in two different ways (e.g. in *Has John money? money* is characterized as an immediate constituent in the surface structure of the sentence, but is considered a part of the predicate phrase in the deep structure). This would be impossible in a taxonomic description.

If our interpretation of Chomsky's distinction between transformational and taxonomic descriptions is correct, we can say that the type of description proposed in this book shares the main features of transformational descriptions, allowing a sufficiently articulated syntactic characterization of the sentence. Since there are two levels of sentence structure in this description, it is possible to characterize a certain item in two ways (it plays in this case a different role on each of the two levels—e.g. that of a goal on the tectogrammatical level, and that of subject on the phenogrammatical level, in a passive sentence), and the symbols of the tectogrammatical level need not be related directly to any subpart of the sentence (cf. Section 4.3.1 for further discussion).

Transformational rules allow permutation and deletion of symbols and addition or insertion of constant strings of symbols.[30] In a description of the type proposed here an addition or insertion of a constant string is, of course, possible, too (as far as we know, in the relevant cases the context criteria can be stated in terms of dependency syntax and represented by rules of pushdown transducers). Deletion of symbols raises questions essentially similar to those connected with deletion in a transformational description (this primarily concerns the recoverability of deletions, which is a necessary condition for the existence of a recognition procedure; cf. Theorem 3 of Chapter 5). Permutation of symbols is possible provided certain restrictions concerning the relative positions of the permuted symbols are met (e.g. two adjacent strings of symbols are permuted one with the other, or a string of symbols is moved to the left of all symbols dependent on its governing symbol, or to the end of the sentence, etc.; cf. the examples concerning such phrases as *větší město než Praha* (*a larger city than Prague*) in Sections 3.4 and 6.3, or the rules concerning the position of prepositions in the fourth transducer of Section 6.3 where a component of a complex symbol is removed, so that, formally, we have to do with the insertion of a constant). On this basis, for instance, rules can be formulated placing the Czech enclitica (like those of the ancient Indo-European languages) just after the first syntagm or word depending on the verb (or after the verb itself, if it is not preceded by any such syntagm).

In some respects, then, the proposed system is more restricted than the transformational description; it is not possible to put one of the permuted (or inserted) symbols into any arbitrarily chosen position in the sentence. But if schemata corresponding to an infinite number of transformations are not used, Chomsky's model is, in a way, similarly restricted. Only after a thorough empirical knowledge of the respective properties of various natural languages has been gained will it be possible to state which of the models is more adequate in this respect.

NOTES

1. In traditional European linguistics, as well as in the immediate-constituent approach, it is usual to consider some types of phrases as connected more closely than others. In traditional terminology, for instance, the connection between an object and its governing verb is considered to be closer than that between an adverbial and the verb, the latter being regarded as closer than the relation between subject and predicate. But examples such as the English *to state beforehand* (if understood as synonymous with *to anticipate*), or the Czech *Včera padal sníh*, which is synonymous with *Včera sněžilo* (both with the meaning *Yesterday it was snowing*, the former sentence corresponding literally to *Yesterday snow was falling*) show that there is no direct connection between this type of "closeness" of syntactic relations and the semantic structure of the given syntagms.
2. For the use of the term "actor", which might appear unusual (at least in some of the examples) in this connection, cf. Section 2.1.3. It is a mere coincidence that the relevant word-forms in our examples are not only actors, but also subjects of their verbs; but if corresponding infinitive or gerund constructions are chosen (e.g. *They prevented the water from flooding the meadow*), it is more or less clear that there exists a unit of a "higher" (or "deeper") level than that of the grammatical structure of the sentence; in a linguistic description a reference to this unit may be necessary to formulate in a simple way, for instance, the rules concerning the distribution of reflexive pronouns.
3. Cf. also the distinction concerning the relative closeness of the dependency relation, as discussed by Kuryłowicz (1948); see also Hausenblas (1958), who points out a direct relationship between the two levels (p. 29) and calls attention to some disproportions between them (pp. 35–37); cf. Note 1, and Section 4.1.2.
4. We would prefer to speak of relations "of type *C*" (or *R*), since they differ according to the particular level concerned.
5. In a somewhat similar way, the relationship between, for example, the semes of accusative, plural, feminine etc. were described by means of logical conjunction by Revzin (1957).
6. In a more detailed elaboration it may be useful, of course, to describe lexical morphemes also by means of more sets of semes.
7. For the use of the term "to realize" (or "realization"), which corresponds in a certain sense to Hockett's term "to represent," cf. Section 1.3.4.
8. Cf. the Russian examples given by Zimmerman (1967) at the end of her paper. Before a concrete set of "actants" can be given, it will be useful to consider what is known from the traditional conceptions about various means conveying distinctions in verbal voice, as well as between intransitive, transitive, and factitive verbs: verbal endings, suffixes, auxiliary verbs, periphrastical constructions with special causative words, etc. Also a confrontation with recent works as for example Halliday (1967) might be of interest, where the "actants," or some of them, are classified within a different theoretical framework.

9. Although many pertinent results can be drawn from Pauliny (1943), dealing with Slovak. For some observations, see Konečná (1966).
10. Cf. Zimmerman (1967); by "regular" we mean expansions of the types *to come somewhere, to behave somehow, to last some time*, etc., which are not necessarily obligatory, but yet required, in a sense, by the verb (their form not being determined by it).
11. Cf. Section 3.1, also Sgall (1967c); in such a case, of course, not a set of sentences, but a set of phonetic realizations of propositions would be specified by the description of language. It would be one of the first steps toward a system that would account for units larger than the sentence; cf. p. 22.
12. On the notions of relation and operation cf. Nebeský and Sgall (1965).
13. The final contour, however, does not always correspond to the end of a sentence (Daneš, 1957, pp. 98f).
14. We differ here from Halle (1959, p. 44f) and others who regard morphophonemes as composed of distinctive features.
15. More precisely, certain subclasses are to be recognized, for example genders of nouns.
16. The term *function of* is used here in the sense of Section 1.3.2, so that it corresponds more or less to Lamb's *realized by*. But in Lamb's system those portions of the description where realization appears in its pure form are called alternation patterns, whereas the so-called sign patterns contain only some special cases of realization together with typical cases of Hockett's relation *C*.
17. Cf. Lamb (1964b, p. 110); there are some inadequacies in Lamb's formulation, which are not relevant in this context; for instance, there remain some optional transformations in the new version of Chomsky's description, accounting for stylistic synonymy and phenomena of a similar kind. We also differ from Lamb in that we do not regard the difference between the "process conception" and the conception of "structural relationships" to be as essential as he assumes (1966b, p. 35). We are not sure that Postal (1964, p. 29) is right in claiming that the difference between Hockett's "item and arrangement" and "item and process" descriptions is a matter of mere terminology, but, unless differences of this kind are formulated as differences between formal systems that can be confronted explicitly, their relevance to the description as a whole remains unclear.
18. The distribution of the English forms used as equivalents is not the same as that of the Czech forms, so that the English translation does not share all the properties concerned here. In Czech the possessive adjective (ending with *-ův*, *-ovo*, etc.) can be used only if there is no adjectival adjunct present.
19. Namely, the formal features specific for natural languages are then characterized by conditions laid on the description (grammar) as such, and not on the respective function assigning structural descriptions to sentences or on a function evaluating the descriptions (cf. point (1a) as against (1c, d) in Chomsky, 1961); cf. now also Chomsky (1965, § 9 of Chapter 1).
20. We do not take into account here questions connected with the relation of coordination.
21. Cf. working principle (i) in Section 2.1.3; Hausenblas (1958), developing the ideas of Kuryłowicz (1948), distinguishes syntactic dependence from semantic determination, the main difference being that the whole phrase is determined by another, while with respect to the dependency relation it is substituted by its head (cf. Section 2.1.1). In the transformational description, deep structure and surface structure, formulated in terms of phrases and their constituents, also share the general form (i.e., they are both rendered by (generalized) P-markers, the underlying and the derived one); expositions of the semantic component (e.g. Katz and Postal, 1964) work with terms such as head and modifier. This shows that it is customary to suppose that the formal properties of the semantic structure of the sentence are closely related to those of the grammatical sentence structure.
22. This proposal was made independently of the corresponding change in the conception of transformational description; cf. Sgall (1964, p. 104).
23. It is a specific characteristic of English that the syntactic role of a constituent can be

frequently specified by its position (e.g. when choosing—by the application of a transformational rule or otherwise—the personal form of a verb one can refer to the preceding *NP* as its subject); but even here it is not so simple in all cases, and for languages such as Czech or Russian (not to speak of Latin, Greek, etc.) it is customary in linguistics to state these contextual conditions in terms of dependence (the form of the modifier often depends in some degree on the head and on the type of dependence, sometimes the form of the head is affected by the type of its modifiers).

24. This treatment is being studied by D. G. Hays (personal communication).
25. It corresponds to the definition of a grammar of this type as a set of rules of the form $a \rightarrow \mathbf{x}$ (where a is a non-terminal symbol and $\mathbf{x}$ a non-null string of symbols); but it is not connected with the notion of a P-marker as a labelled tree.
26. Furthermore, in the output strings of this transducer the functors are no longer differentiated by means of indices; special suffixes (indices) are attached now to every dependent symbol (by means of the mapping $\mathbf{q}_1$; cf. Section 6.4), which correspond to the different kinds of dependence, that is, to the sentence parts.
27. One of the tasks of the fourth transducer should be to change the functors into boundary symbols from which at the end symbols corresponding to phonetic pauses could be derived. We do not attempt to solve questions of intonation here; hence in Chapters 5 and 6 automaton $\mathbf{T}_4$ is presented without satisfying requirements of this kind.
28. Several propositions (differing in the closeness of some of the syntactic pairs) correspond to this tree.
29. This string can be excluded if nouns are classified as to animateness by the generative component. The rules included in our illustrations would not exclude such a string, but this is due to their preliminary character. Furthermore, it is an open question whether such a string should not be excluded on the phenogrammatical level, too; according to Chomsky (1957, § 7.5) such strings are ungrammatical.
30. Cf. Chomsky (1961); attachment transformations are not considered here, since in the new version of transformational description they are replaced by rules of the base.

3. ILLUSTRATIONS

3.1 SENTENCE TYPES

The generative component of the description generates the representations of sentences on the tectogrammatical level (the propositions) as formulae of the simple "language" characterized in a preliminary way in Chapter 2 (for a formal specification see Chapter 5). Several alternative approaches are perhaps possible, for example those using some modification of predicate calculus (for one of them see Čulík, 1965a, pp. 230ff, 1965b, pp. 284–287). In any case, these approaches are meant as a generative specification of semantic representations of sentences; this view, which was confined to a small group of linguists three or four years ago, is now widely accepted. But those who have some experience of these views may warn its more recent adherents against some dangerous simplifications. First, semantics is a vast and unexplored field, which probably cannot be accounted for by a single level (see Section 2.1.1 for the distinction between content and meaning, and Section 4.2 for other open questions); second, the relationship between semantics and syntax (in a natural language) is far from clear (for our standpoint, see Section 1.3); and, third, there are no convincing arguments for semantic interpretations being universal (if meaning and not content is taken as the object of linguistic study).

We give here several tentative illustrations concerning the generative specification of semantic interpretations of syntactic constructions and of morphological items, without trying to enter the area of lexical semantics. If the description is to generate all types of sentences (and also certain sequences of sentences; cf. Section 2.1.3), then at least the four following matters must be dealt with:

(I) the types of syntactic iteration that are to be accounted for by recursion in the generative component;
(II) sentence types as differentiated by sentence modality;
(III) sentence types as differentiated by the main member of the sentence (two-member and one-member—nominal or verbal—sentences);
(IV) possibilities of coordination and other combinations of sentences belonging to different types.

Of course, the first component generates tectogrammatical representations of sentences, that is, also representations of sequences of sentences that are synonymous with single sentences. One then has to speak of types of propositions and to examine whether there are any substantial differences as to points (II) and (III) between these types of propositions and the sentence types of traditional grammars.

In our generative component, expansion rules and selectional rules are distinguished clearly by their form (cf. Section 6.2; a selectional rule can be defined as a rule the application of which leads to no change of the derived string other than replacing a non-terminal symbol by a terminal; other rules of this component are expansion rules); the rules of this component are unordered. If we assume with Chomsky (1957, § 3.3 and also 1965, p. 8) that recursion must be taken into account for an adequate and simple description, then it is useful to ensure the recursive character of this component by the set of expansion rules. It is necessary to work with at least two types of recursion; as far as we know, no Czech sentence can be offered as the longest Czech sentence possible (and this also applies to propositions), because (a) some of its parts can always be expanded by another dependent predication[1] and (b) a further counterpart, coordinated with it (or standing in apposition), can always be added to the whole sentence or to some of its parts. Thus predicative and coordinative recursions can be distinguished. Other types of recursion, the necessity of which has not yet been proved for the Czech language, are not discussed here.[2]

In the new version of Chomsky's transformational description the two types of recursion are provided for by means of the recursive symbol *S*, which serves at the same time as the initial symbol (we abstract here from the boundary symbols as parts of the initial string). But it is not necessary that the recursive symbol be identical with the initial one; certain facts seem to give evidence for another solution. Let us take the following Czech sentences to illustrate point (IV) above:

(1) *Ty se tam podívej a já počkám tady.* (*Have a look there, and I shall wait here.*)

(2) *Já zůstanu tady, ale kéž by Karel šel domů.* (*I shall stay here, but if only Charles would go home!*)

(3) *Prší a Karel nepřichází.* (*It is raining, and Charles does not come.*)

(4) *Karel nepřijde, protože prší.* (*Charles will not come, because it is raining.*)

(5) *Jé, mami, to nemyslíš vážně!* (*Oh, mother, you can't mean that!*)

On the other hand, there are no Czech sentences such as:

(6) *Přijď domů a zůstaneš tam dlouho?* (*Come home and will you stay there long?*)

(7) *Zůstanu tady, protože kéž by přišel.* (*I shall stay here, for would he only come.*)

(8) *Zůstanu tady, protože přijď.* (*I shall stay here, because come* (imperative).)

(9) *Dávej pozor, protože auto!* (*Be careful, because a car!*)

The examples show that in some cases two predications belonging to different kinds of so-called sentence modality can be coordinated—as in (1) and (2)—but in other cases this is not possible—as in (6). And, furthermore, it is not possible to embed an imperative (8) or desiderative (7) predication into any proposition, that is these kinds of modality do not occur in dependent predications. Cases such as *Řekli mu, ať to udělá* (*They told him to do it*) are of a specific kind; their description is to be formulated in connection with that of direct and indirect discourse. As to indirect questions, this applies, too; one type is discussed in Section 3.2. Leaving these cases aside, we can say that the distinction between declarative, interrogative, desiderative, and imperative[3] concerns the main predication only, not the dependent. This can be formalized by distinguishing the symbol for proposition (with indices of various modalities) from the symbol of predication (dependent or not), so that independent predication would be derived directly from proposition, but dependent predication would be introduced by another rule (as an expansion of its governing symbol).

But taking into consideration the possibilities of coordination, one has to admit that the distinction between symbols for proposition and predication will not suffice. However, it is possible to formulate a set of rules such as (a) to (f),[4] which admits (1) and (2), but excludes (6) as well as (7) and (8):

(a) $Proposition \longrightarrow \left\{ \begin{array}{l} Declar \\ Interr \end{array} \right.$

(b) $Declar \longrightarrow \left\{ \begin{array}{l} Pred_{enunc} \\ Pred_{desid} \\ Pred_{imper} \end{array} \right.$

(c) $Interr \longrightarrow Pred_{interr}$

(d) $X \longrightarrow X \quad X \quad R_c$ where *X* stands for *Declar* and *Interr*

(e) $Pred_{modal} \longrightarrow NP \quad VP_{modal} \; R_a$ where *modal* stands for *enunc, desid, imper*[5]

(f) $NP \longrightarrow \left\{ \begin{array}{l} N \\ Pred \end{array} \right.$

There is another problem connected with sentence modality, that is with point (II). Given rule (c) as formulated above, the structure of an interrogative proposition would be the same as that of a declarative one, with the only difference concerning the index of sentence modality. This can account well for *yes-no* questions. If *wh*-questions are to be provided for, another symbol would be necessary besides *Pred;* the expansion rules of such a symbol would be to a great extent similar to those of *Pred*, except for the fact that the terminal string derived in that way would contain one or more interrogative semantemes. A deeper elaboration along these lines (which should be parallel in many points to that formulated for English by Katz and Postal, 1964)[6] would presuppose an investigation of further distributional features of interrogative semantemes (of the possibilities of their expansion, etc.). These features can be examined along with similar problems concerning indefinite and relative pronouns and indirect questions; the description should take advantage of certain similarities of the distributional features of types mentioned above. In this book only *yes-no* questions are taken into account; indirect questions are provided for only with one group of verbs (as their goal), and relative attributive sentences are described with some simplifications (cf. Section 3.3 and the rules given in Section 6.2).

Coming now to point (III), we should like to remark that the so-called one-member sentences should also be considered in the description. As to the verbal sentences (and propositions), for example *Svítá* (*It is dawning*; cf. Russ. *Svetajet*) or *Prší* (*It is raining*), the task is relatively simple; they can be coordinated with two-member propositions or embedded into them—cf. (3) and (4)—and so their verbs can be derived without difficulty from a symbol for predication; cf. Rule 30 in Section 6.2. But there are problems concerning other types of one-member sentences; sometimes they are regarded as non-sentential utterances, whereas some linguists make a distinction between nominal sentences ("expressions of judgments", adopting a certain standpoint to a given situation etc., cf. Kopečný, 1962) and so-called sentential equivalents (emotional nominatives, vocatives, interjections).[7] It is necessary, for a detailed description, to study these questions in connection with those concerning the relationship of exclamatory sentences to other types (cf. Note 3). Here we modify rules (a), (b) in such a way as to provide also for "sentential equivalents" so that they cannot be embedded into a predication, cf. the impossibility of (9); but some of them—interjections and vocatives—can form a part of a regular sentence, cf. (5); their position is then that of a "separate sentence part" (cf. e.g. Šmilauer, 1947), which is rendered here by a special functor, R_v; cf. Rules 1 to 5 in Section 6.2, where propositions realized by "sentential equivalents" are formally characterized in that they are derived without the use of the symbol *Pred.*

There are further special problems connected with the syntax of vocatives. Not only can they not be coordinated with any other type of proposition, but also their occurrence inside other propositions is restricted by conditions which have to be respected in the description.

The description should

(a) admit such sentences as

Táto, přijď brzo! (*Father, come*(*sg*) *early!*) *Táto, přijďte* (*s mámou*) *brzo!* (*Father, come* (pl) (*with mother*) *early!*) *Táto, přišel jsi brzo.* (*Father, you have come early.*) *Táto, máma přišla.* (*Father, mother has come.*) *Táto, ti lidé odcházejí.* (*Father, the people are going away.*) *Děti, ať je tu ticho!* (*Children, there must be quiet here*!)

(b) exclude such strings as

Děti, přijď brzo! (*Children, come* (*sg*) *early!*) *Táto a mámo, přijď brzo!* (*Father and mother, come* (sg) *early!*) *Děti, máš špinavou košili.* (*Children, you have* (sg) *a dirty shirt.*)

If the main verb of a sentence containing a vocative form is in the second person singular, then the vocative form cannot be in the plural, nor can there be several coordinated vocative forms. The relation between a sentence in the third person and that in the second person could be regarded, in some sense, as a transformation; then the subject of the sentence (if it is not a personal pronoun), or perhaps one of the members of a subject formed by coordination, must be transformed into the vocative form. In the present version of the transformational grammar, however, where transformations should not change the meaning of the sentence, this distinction of persons must be accounted for in the base. This is also the case for our type of description, where the distinction of persons must already be provided for on the tectogrammatical level. Moreover, it should be noted that the said properties of the second person and its combination with vocative forms concern subordinate clauses as well. Thus it is necessary to formulate a set of rules by the application of which the symbol *Pred* (with a subscript) can be rewritten in two ways: either as a symbol of the second person (denoted as $Pred_2$ in Rule 5 of Section 6.2), or as the symbol $Pred_1$, from which the constructions with the first and third persons are gained (according to the semantics of the subject); the symbol $Pred_1$ can be combined with a vocative clause by the means of the functor R_v; cf. the quoted rule. If the symbol $Pred_2$ is chosen, then the actor is realized by a vocative form; cf. Table 2, Section 6.4.

3.2 THE STRUCTURE OF SENTENCES

As has been pointed out in Section 2.1.3, we work in our illustrations with units such as actor, goal and free modification of various types; they are conceived as different kinds of dependency relations (the types of modification are distinguished by suffixes). Further, two points (closely connected with each other) are taken into account in the description of the verb and its various expansions: First, allowance is made for the derivation of various orders for such expansions (either directly on the tectogrammatical level, or —for some derived variants of word order—in the course of the transduction). Second, the fact that individual types of dependent members differ in degree of closeness of their relation to the verb is respected. The former point is brought about by the free character of the Czech word order. There is another possibility of handling this feature of Czech, namely to restrict the recursive component of the generative description to the specification of strings with a basic word order only, and to provide for its possible alteration in the other components. However, we do not suppose this approach to be suitable for the description of Czech, since, at least in some cases (inside the verbal phrase, in syntagms consisting of a verb and its actor or adverbial modifier) the order of lexical elements is given by factors belonging mainly to functional sentence perspective (topic-comment articulation), which is closely connected with the semantics of the sentence (cf. Section 4.2.1 and Sgall, 1967b) and is to be accounted for at the tectogrammatical level.

It is necessary to derive, at this level, at least the following variants (differing as to the positions of actor and goal):

(i) *Karel vás uvidí.*
(ii) *Karel uvidí vás.*
(iii) *Vás uvidí Karel.*
(iv) *Uvidí vás Karel.*

} (*Charles will see you.*)

If these sentences are pronounced with a neutral intonation, then only (i) can be used as an answer to the question (v), only (ii) to (vi), only (iii) to (vii), and (iv) to (viii):

(v) *Uvidí vás Karel?* (*Will Charles see you?*)

(vi) *Koho uvidí Karel?* (*Whom will Charles see?*)

(vii) *Kdo uvidí vás?* (*Who will see you?*)—as contrasted with *Kdo uvidí Pavla?* (*Who will see Paul?*)

(viii) *Kdo vás uvidí?* (*Who will see you?*)—*as* contrasted with *Kdo vás neuvidí?* (*Who will not see you?*)

Further, variants of the shape *NP VP Adv*, *Adv NP VP*, etc. also should be generated at the tectogrammatical level.

To achieve this,[8] we use rules of two forms:

(a) $X \longrightarrow Y \quad Z \quad R$

(b) $X \longrightarrow Z \quad Y \quad R'$

where *X*, *Y*, *Z* are non-terminal symbols and *R* is a functor; a functor without prime is interpreted as denoting the dependence of the left-hand non-terminal symbol on the right, that is, of *Y* on *Z* in (a), whereas a functor with prime denotes dependence in the reverse direction, that is of the right-hand symbol on the left (of *Y* on *Z* in (b)). To avoid (at least for the informal presentation) the necessity of repeating many rules in both forms, we accept the following convention: whenever a rule of the form (a)—or (b)—is listed in the grammar, there exists also the corresponding rule of the form (b)—or (a)—where *X* is a non-terminal symbol other than *NP*, *Nom*, *Adv*. (This restriction is due to the fact that some rules for adnominal free modification and for the expansion of adverbs admit one order only.[9]) Also in the terminal string, that is in the proposition, this interpretation is retained; if the functors are regarded as functors of two arguments in a parenthesis-free notation, then the prime at the functor indicates that the leftmost of its arguments is the governor of the phrase, whereas a functor without prime indicates the rightmost of the arguments as the governor (the order "*regens post rectum*").

The syntagm actor–verb is considered here to be relatively loose, similarly as in many other types of description (but cf. Section 2.1.1 and 2.2.3). The symbol *Pred* is therefore rewritten as an impersonal verb (cf. Rule 30 in the list of rules, Section 6.2) or as a syntagm composed of a *NP* in the position of actor and of a predicate phrase (verbal, nominal or quantitative; cf. Rules 6, 7 in the said list). Each of these kinds of predicate phrase is expanded by further rules.

The suffixes—written as indices of complex symbols in our notation—are chosen only to illustrate how it would be possible to account in the description for the morphological semantemes (cf. Section 2.1.3). Our preliminary examples of rules do not exclude many of their combinations that should be excluded as a matter of course (e.g. those of perfective aspect and present tense, or of imperative modality with preterit); as has been said in Section 1.2, we are not attempting to give a grammar specifying only Czech sentences, since we are aware that it is a difficult task to find all the empirical restrictions that have not yet been studied systematically. It will be necessary, in further elaboration, to formulate a far more complete list of suffixes (especially those of the type "modif"), and, probably, to provide for a hierarchy among them (or, at least, among some of them); cf. now Panevová (in prep.) for suffixes of tense, relative tense, and aspect, Komrsková (1967) for those of cause and condition, Havelková (1968) for modal suffixes, Piťha (in press) for those of place.

The strings derived by the application of the last two lines of Rule 5 correspond to propositions with the so-called general subject (actor), such as *Říkají mu Karel* (*They call him Charles*), or *Člověk nikdy neví* (*One never knows*); cf. Havránek (1928, p. 16) as to the relationship of actor and subject in these cases.

The term "goal" refers to the type of complement that is obligatory[10] and the form of which is determined by its governor; sometimes it is not determined uniquely, but then either synonymy is present, as for example *záviset na—záviset od* (*to depend on*), or the forms are distinguished semantically, as *ukázat na něco—ukázat něco* (*to point to something—to show something;* cf. the German *auf etwas zeigen—etwas zeigen*). An obligatory complement the form of which is not determined by its governor (sometimes called a complementary adverbial, as contrasted with a qualifying adverbial, e.g. Šmilauer, 1947, p. 257), must be generated by specific rules, but it conforms with the optional (qualifying) expansion in both its semantics and its form. This obligatory adverbial is always defined semantically: for example with *chovat se* (*to behave*) it is an adverbial of manner, with *octnout se* (*to find o.s. in*), *usídlit se*, (*to establish o.s.*) an adverbial of place, with *odebrat se* (*to depart for*), *směřovat* (*to aim at*) an adverbial of direction; cf. Rules 10, 35 to 37 in Section 6.2. The indirect question is provided for as a goal of a special kind (Rules 10 and 11).

Two obligatory complements with verbs such as *volit za* (*to elect*) are regarded as two types of goal: the first becomes a subject if the verb is in the passive and it is derived by Rule 12, while the other is derived as a "goal complement" according to the third line in Rule 10. With the type *soutěžit, prát se s někým o něco* (*to compete, to fight with someone for something*) etc. the so-called impersonal object is regarded as a goal, and the so-called personal object as a qualifying (optional) adverbial.[11]

The so-called indirect object is treated here as a qualifying adverbial; verbs like *přát někomu něco* (*to wish somebody something*) could be treated similarly as *volit za* (cf. above). This solution would also be possible with verbs such as *učit někoho něco* (*něčemu*) (*to teach somebody something*).

The "compound predicate"[12] has been treated in Sgall (1967a) according to the views known especially from the works of Havránek (e.g. Havránek and Jedlička, 1963), that is, it has been represented by a single word on the tectogrammatical level. In the present book the copula is handled as a separate word at the tectogrammatical level, since this makes it possible to provide for morphological semantemes belonging to the predication as a whole (and not to the predicative nominal alone) in a relatively simple way. As to modal verbs we assume that it will be possible to determine—on the basis of syntactic criteria—those units that can be represented on the tectogrammatical level as suffixes attached to the head of predication, though they are represented by a separate word on the lower levels. (For a detailed discussion, cf. Havelková, 1968; Benešová, in press.)

As an example of such a suffix the verb *moci* (*can, may, to be possible*) may be quoted, which meets the necessary requirements mentioned above. It has no tense and aspect of its own differing from those of the main verb, it does not exhibit any special syntactic relations to other sentence parts: the whole construction *moci*+infinitive has a single actor, and (as far as the distinction of meaning is concerned) even the goal or the free modification does not need to be divided into those belonging to the infinitive and to the modal verb. Only such pairs as *Josef to dobře nemůže udělat—Josef to nemůže udělat dobře* (*Joseph cannot well do it—Joseph cannot do it well*) or *Mohu tam nejít—Nemohu tam jít* (*I am able not to go there—I am not able to go there*) indicate that more delicate devices for the description are needed. However, they do not make any change of the basic approach necessary, since units with such general meaning as for example *dobře* (*well*) (in such a phrase as *dobře nemůže —he can't well*) may also be represented on the tectogrammatical level as suffixes; as to negation, see Benešová (in press). The procedure suggested here also leads to an acceptable representation of the relation between active and passive constructions in Czech: *Jan může spatřit Karla—Karel může být spatřen Janem* (*It is possible that John sees Charles—It is possible that Charles is seen by John*; cf. the German *Johann kann Karl sehen—Karl kann von Johann gesehen werden*): on the tectogrammatical level there is a single representation of sentences differing in that one is in active and the other in passive form, and the sentences with *moci* are actually synonymous.

On the other hand the verb *chtít* (*to want, to wish*) cannot be represented so easily by a modal suffix, at least in some of its meanings and syntactic functions. This concerns the construction *Chci, aby zítra přišel* (*I want him to come tomorrow*) with various tenses and actors; when the actor is the same in both clauses, then the question arises whether the sentence *Chci, abych tam zítra byl včas* (*I wish I'll be there in time tomorrow*) is fully or partly synonymous with the sentence *Chci tam zítra být včas* (*I want to be there in time tomorrow*). Thus the verb *chtít* must be—for some constructions—handled as an independent lexical unit (which would be expanded by the infinitive as its goal). Moreover, the sentence *Karel chce být spatřen Janem* (*Charles wants to be seen by John*) cannot be regarded as a passive representation of the proposition the active form of which is *Jan chce spatřit Karla* (*John wants to see Charles*). If "volitive" is treated as one of the verbal "moods," then in the course of transduction to the level of sentence parts there must be a restriction ensuring that the predicate with volitive is not transformed into the passive form (see Table 2 in Section 6.4).

3.3 OPTIONAL SENTENCE PARTS

On the tectogrammatical level, free modification can be classified into two types according to whether it modifies a noun phrase or some other type of phrase. This corresponds to the customary distinction on the phenogrammatical level: the former type is realized, primarily, by the attributive, while the latter by the adverbial (though in some particular contexts both types of free modification may be realized by some other type of sentence part).

In generative (esp. in transformational) descriptions, the attributive is usually accounted for in a direct relationship to the predicate. The relation between such pairs as *the table is old* and *the old table*, or *the table that is old* was, of course, recognized long before transformational grammar existed. However, the direction of this relation was understood in different ways: while for example Kuryłowicz (1936) regards the attributive construction as the primary one, the transformational grammars consider the attributive to be a secondary modification of the predicative syntagm (elsewhere the notion of depredication is employed for such cases). Here we follow the latter direction, regarding the predicative construction to be primary, since we find it convenient to start in the description of the sentence structure with the form of an overt predication, from which other constructions would be derived.

Thus, on the tectogrammatical level, such a rule as Rule 19 of Section 6.2 can reflect the relationship between the predicate and the attributive, in that a predicative syntagm will be then derived from the symbol *Pred*. This way of treating the attributive may be taken as a common basis both for the relative clause and for the simple attributive (in the former case, the occurrence of the noun in the expanding phrase is substituted by a relative pronoun, while in the latter it is omitted).

This treatment of the attributive has, however, various shortcomings; some of these can be removed relatively easily, while for an adequate solution of the others a further elaboration will be necessary:

(a) Such attributes as *každý* (*every*), *ten* (*this*), *pouhý* (*mere*) cannot be derived from the symbol *Pred*. For the first two (that is for the types, for which these examples stand) special rules must be added (cf. Rules 17, 18 in Section 6.2); the construction *pouhý bod* (*a mere point*) can be regarded as synonymous with *jen bod* (*only a point*), so that they will have a single representation at the tectogrammatical level (cf. Rule 15). Rule 16 makes it possible to rewrite the symbol *NP* as *Pred*, that is, to give the nominal phrase the form of dependent predication (cf. Section 3.1 on predicative recursion), and at the same time a suffix for the relative tense (simultaneous, preceding, succeeding) is added to the symbol *Pred* (but now see Panevová, in preparation).

(b) Furthermore, the rules in question do not account for the restriction in the opposite direction, namely that not every predicative relation can be changed (transformed, depredicated) into an attributive. The necessary restrictions are not provided for by Rule 19. An examination should be made of whether these restrictions concern the tectogrammatical level or only the transduction to the lower levels: For instance, in *bratr, který je chytrý chlapec* (*brother who is a clever boy*) the attributive must be realized by a clause at the lower levels; on the other hand there are such constructions as *zvonek, který je v předsíni* (*the bell that is in the hall*), for which the synonymous construction does exist—*zvonek v předsíni* (*the bell in the hall*). Another question remaining open concerns the requirement that the adnominal predication must contain an occurrence of the noun on which it depends. The new conception of transformational grammar reckons with such a condition (cf. Chomsky, 1965). This approach, however, does not take into account cases where the underlying P-marker of the embedded phrase contains several occurrences of the word that is identical with the governing noun. The transformational rules would then lead to several different sentences (according to which one of these occurrences would be deleted or changed into a relative word). In the transformational description these sentences would be characterized as synonymous (for the most part unjustifiably) because they would correspond to a single string generated by the base (with the same underlying phrase marker). The description must be supplied by an indication of the particular occurrence of the word-form in the embedded phrase that refers to the governing noun; but this concerns another question, see point (c) below.

Before we pass to it, we must ask whether the stated condition is necessary. Are there not adnominal modifications that do not include a word identical with the governing noun? Our point can be illustrated by sentences such as *Přinesli takový stůl, že místnost je hned malá* (*They brought such a table that the room immediately looks small*) or *Takové počasí, abychom se* (*že jsme se*) *koupali v řece, bylo letos jen týden* (*Only for a week this year was such weather that we could bath in the river*). The word *takový* (*such*) is usually regarded in other cases as "referential" (cf. Šmilauer, 1947, p. 163), that is as a function word without lexical meaning of its own, which only points to a clause. With this treatment of *takový* the dependent clause should be regarded as an adnominal phrase. Even then the given examples could be characterized as sentences where the dependent predication (the embedded phrase) includes a word identical with the governing noun, implying for instance, that the tectogrammatical representation of the dependent predication in the second example would be regarded as a string corresponding to the graphic representation *Počasí bylo takové, že jsme se koupali v řece* (*The weather was such that we bathed in the river*). However, it is not certain whether insertion of a further dependent predication is necessary. For this reason we do not insert a restriction in Rule 19.

(c) The sense of the Czech phrases *starý stůl* (*an old table*) and *stůl, který je starý* (*a table that is old*) can be accounted for in several different ways, but in any case the representation should account for the fact that the word *který* (*that*) refers to the word *stůl* (*table*), that is, that they both denote the same object. (This is also true of the simple attributive, where there is no special word for such a reference.) In our representation at the tectogrammatical level—*stůl stůl starý* R_a R'_a—the double occurrence of the semanteme *stůl* (*table*) does not account for identity of reference (referential meaning), but it points to identity of meaning, which could hardly be understood directly from the given Czech phrases (if we do not assume that it directly follows from identity of reference, which need not hold in general).

The requirement that the identity of reference should be taken into account does not concern the relative words alone, but the anaphorical means as well. Since the description proposed here provides no solution for questions of referential meaning (cf. Section 2.1.3), it would be premature to assume that an adequate way of dealing with identity of reference could be added in a simple way; Sgall (1967a) makes some suggestions.

(d) The rule above does not exclude noun phrases such as *starý nový stůl* (*an old new table*); *starý starý stůl, který je nový* (*an old old table that is new*), which should obviously be ruled out by a full description of Czech. As far as we know, difficulties of this kind have not yet been overcome in any other type of generative description. They can be solved only on the basis of a detailed description of the hierarchy of lexical elements.

A similar problem arises with modification of the type represented on the phenogrammatical level by an adverbial. It is equally evident here that strings such as *Loni se včera učil* (*Last year he learned yesterday*), or *V Africe se pěstuje pšenice hlavně v Asii* (*In Africa wheat is grown especially in Asia*) should not be regarded as grammatical sentences. Algebraic linguistics follows here the previous endeavour to divide adverbial modification into types that may—as distinct modifications of the same word, not standing in coordination or apposition—combine only with each other (cf. the so-called types of adverbials in the works of Šmilauer; in connection with machine translation, a similar standpoint is adopted e.g. by Pashchenko, 1965a, 1965b). Taking this view, we should then see in sentences such as *V Africe se pěstuje pšenice hlavně v mírném pásmu* (*In Africa wheat is grown especially in the mild zone*), which is certainly grammatically correct and meaningful, an apposition of two adverbial modifications of the same type, divided into two distinct positions in the sentence, just as the noun phrase is split in sentences like *Sportovec on je dobrý* (*As a sportsman he is good*).[13] But such a splitting is conditioned by special features of functional sentence perspective, and there are examples such as *Včera se večer učil doma* (*Yesterday he studied in the evening at home*), where these features hardly could be found. Furthermore, there are types of adverbials that certainly can occur at least twice in a sentence, one occurrence being connected with the whole phrase containing the other; this is, for instance, the case of adverbials of cause: for example *Přišel jsem pozdě kvůli dešti, protože jsem neměl s sebou deštník* (*I came late due to the rain, because I had not my umbrella with me*); cf. Komrsková (1968). Therefore we keep here to the treatment shown by the recursive Rule 25; the problem should be solved perhaps with the same means as in the case of unacceptable attributive strings.

There exist, of course, many other restrictions of free modification, only some of which are treated here.

Rules 26 and 27 prevent our deriving such strings as *Včera přijdu* (*Yesterday I'll come*). Also the rules for the mutual expansion of adverbs

(Rules 21–24) are more fully specified than those concerning other word classes.

Negation could also be accounted for as a free modification; it is not, however, included in our examples, because we need to examine the problem of representing different types of negation in a uniform way (with the necessary restrictions), and at the same time to respect its special semantic nature (e.g. also the synonymy of Czech sentences *Nemusím přijít—Mohu nepřijít* (*I need not come—I am allowed not to come*), cf. Havelková (1968).

3.4 TRANSDUCTION

For the most part, the changes connected with the transition from the tectogrammatical or phenogrammatical level to the next lower one consist (speaking intuitively) in that individual word-form tokens (occurring in the representation of the sentence on the higher level) are changed according to conditions given by:[14]

(a) meaning (semantic function) and syntactic class (category) of the word itself;

(b) its syntactic function, that is, its relation to the word governing it;

(c) semantic and syntactic functions of words depending on the given word;

(d) the form class of the governing word;

(e) stylistic criteria.

There are, of course, other cases (i.e., cases where the difference between the representations of a given sentence on two adjacent levels are of a more complicated nature, or where the corresponding change of a word-form token is conditioned by other criteria), but these are not so typical for natural languages as those mentioned above. Let us first give some examples of the typical changes and conditions, to show how they can be described by the chosen formal devices.

The transition from tectogrammatics to phenogrammatics can be characterized by changes corresponding to Kuryłowicz's *dérivation syntaxique* (by the choice between a dependent clause and a nominalization, or "condensation;" see Vachek, 1955, 1961), and also by the choice between active and passive. A Czech sentence like (1) has several paraphrases differing in their representations on the phenogrammatical level, for example (2), (3).

(1) *Kdyby někdo zpozoroval, že se o to snažíš, věděli bychom to.* (*If someone noticed that you strove for that, we should know about it.*)

(2) *Kdyby někdo zpozoroval tvou snahu o to, věděli bychom to.* (*If someone noticed your striving for that, we . . .*)

(3) *Kdyby byla zpozorována tvá snaha o to, věděli bychom to.* (*If your striving for that were noticed by someone, we . . .*)

The distinction between (1) and (2) consists in a nominalization against a dependent clause; the choice is conditioned here by the verbal semantemes belonging to a certain class—the class of verbal semantemes that can be nominalized, a condition of type (a)—and by some stylistic conditions (e); the conditions of type (e) are regarded here solely as free variations (cf. Table 2 in Section 6.4). The distinction between (2) and (3), that is that between active and passive, is connected with a choice based on conditions of the same two groups, but a more comprehensive treatment of stylistic phenomena would have to take account of conditions of type (c), too, since in Czech the passive construction is far more frequent with verbs having a general actor (which can be translated by the English *one*) than with verbs having a special actor (be it a noun, a pronoun, or a verb).

In some cases the possibility of a nominalization is limited by a condition of type (b); sentence (1), for instance, cannot be paraphrased by nominalizing its first clause (which depends on the main verb as an unreal condition, i.e., one of the specific types of free modification; see the list in Section 6.2). Before a systematic description of such conditions can be formulated (which would make it possible to specify in detail the mapping $\mathbf{t}_2$ of Section 5.2 or Table 2 of Section 6.4), large-scale empirical investigation is necessary. Besides that, the description has to reflect the fact that generally nominalizations are not fully synonymous with clauses, since they are connected with different degrees of reduction of morphological categories (cf. Jelínek, 1965, 1966).

Furthermore, the phenogrammatical representation of a sentence differs from tectogrammatical representation in certain more technical respects; some changes of symbols are conditioned by a criterion of type (d), for instance, an actor turning into subject (if the active form of the governing verb has been chosen), or into a special type of adverbial modification (with the governing verb in the passive), or into attributive (if the verb has been nominalized).

Conditions of choice belonging to types (a) to (d)—as well as (e), if regarded as free variation only—can be accounted for by transducing devices of the form given in Chapter 5. The functioning of the transducers can be interpreted in such a way that the first of them writes down the governing symbol in the output only after confronting it with all the symbols that depend on it and after changing it accordingly (cf. the mapping $\mathbf{t}_1$; cf. also Note 26 to Chapter 2), whenever there is a possibility that conditions of type (c) will be needed later. The second transducer reads the governing symbol first, changes it into a corresponding symbol of the phenogrammatical level (cf. the mapping $\mathbf{t}_2$ and rules such as 2, 6–10 in the transducer $\mathbf{T}_2$ in Section 5.2) using criteria of types (a), (b)—that is, criteria based on items given by the form of the changed complex symbol itself. After this, it confronts this symbol with those dependent on it and changes them according to conditions of the type mentioned, and to those of type (d).

In the course of the transition from the phenogrammatical representation to the morphemic, the dependent symbols are changed according to the categories of rection and concord—that is, to criteria of types (a), (b) and (d)—by the fourth transducer, in a manner essentially similar to the functioning of the second transducer (cf. the mapping $\mathbf{t}_4$ and the example, Section 6.5). When a condition of type (c) is needed for this transition, the corresponding changes of the symbol can be provided by the third transducer. Subordinating conjunctions and prepositions, which figure only as components of complex symbols on the higher levels, are changed into autonomous symbols (i.e., words of the morphemic level) and are placed at the beginning of the respective phrases by the fourth transducer.

So the distinction between independent lexical units (represented as words on each level) and the so-called grammatical words (represented as words on the morphemic and lower levels only) is modelled by a description of the proposed type: as to their role in the semantic and syntactic structure of the sentence, these grammatical words are handled similarly to endings or suffixes, but they differ in their morphemic shape. For instance, the synonymy of Czech *Šli přes les* and *Šli lesem* (*They went through the forest*) can be accounted for (where the construction of the preposition *přes* with the accusative case is synonymous with the instrumental); both these phrases will have the same representation on the phenogrammatical level.

Changes limited by conditions of the types mentioned are typical for many natural languages, and we tried to choose the formal components of the description so as to make it possible to model these types in a relatively simple manner; transducers of the basic form described in Chapter 5 meet this requirement. But, as was noted at the beginning of this section, in individual languages there are also changes of more specific kinds: changes that do not affect a single symbol only, or are connected with more complex criteria. Some of these are illustrated by the example in Section 6.5; here we give only a short informal comment.

In Czech, for instance, as in Russian, the construction of a noun with a numeral higher than *four* (and with some numeral pronouns) can be represented on the phenogrammatical level by a syntagm of the type *Numeral Noun-attr*, that is the noun (standing to the right) is handled as an attributive of the numeral (in this way, the phenomenon of concord, i.e. the transition to the morphemic level, can be described in a relatively simple manner). But on the tectogrammatical level, a phrase such as *pět knih* (*five books*, cf. the Russian *pjat' knig*) has to be represented in the same way as *čtyři knihy* (*four books*, *četyre knigi*); here the numeral is treated similarly as other adnominal modifications. This change in the orientation of the dependency relation can be provided by one of the transducers (Rules 26, 28 of $\mathbf{T}_2$ in Section 6.3).

Moreover, in Czech as in other European languages, a phrase consisting of a noun and its adjectival attributive (on the phenogrammatical level) should be described, in most cases, as synonymous with a noun governing a certain relative clause (cf. Section 3.3). In a system of the proposed type, phrases such as Cz. *velký stůl* (*large table*) and *stůl, který je velký* (*table that is large*) differ at the tectogrammatical level only in the order of symbols. In the transition to the phenogrammatical representation, it is necessary to delete the copula and the symbol of the noun inside the relative clause, if the attributive is not to have the form of a clause; this is provided by rules 22 to 31 of transducer $\mathbf{T}_2$ and Rules 11–13 of $\mathbf{T}_1$ (see Section 6.3), which make this optional change possible only if the noun inside the relative clause does not govern any other symbol. (However, not all the word-order conditions are provided for in our examples in Chapter 6.)

Another example of changes that cannot be provided for by transducers of the basic form is seen in transducer T_4 (Section 6.3). A Czech phrase such as *větší město než Praha* (*a larger city than Prague*) probably cannot be described by a dependency grammar in any other way than with the prepositional phrase *než Praha* depending on the adjective *větší*, which itself depends on the noun *město*. But such a dependency structure, with the given word order, would not fulfill the condition of projectivity, and it could not be represented properly by a linear formula of the type used here. The word order is conditioned by the grammatical properties of the phrase; the string *větší než Praha město* is not a constituent of any grammatical sentence. It is possible to assign the latter order to the tectogrammatical and phenogrammatical representations of the given phrase, and to reverse the order of *než Praha* and *město* in the transition to the morphemic level. Since there are strong restrictions as to the length of such phrases, no essential enlargement of the generative power of the transducer is necessary.

NOTES

1. For the use of the term "predication", cf. p. 50 and also the position of the symbol *Pred* in the set of rules (Section 6.2).
2. In Czech, as in other languages, there exists a recursion in connection with direct discourse; the goal of the introductory verb has the form not of a mere predication, nor of a sentence, but of a higher unit, which is not provided for by the existing forms of linguistic description, and which itself may contain another introductory sentence connected with direct discourse.
3. Exclamatory sentences should probably be considered as constituting a fifth type, even if their syntactic shape is identical with that of questions (*Cos to tu udělal!—What have you done here!*), declarative sentences (*Tak tady jsi!—So here you are!*), etc., if we disregard their intonation. They are characterized semantically.
4. Abbreviations with initial capital letters are non-terminal symbols, or parts of such symbols (in complex symbols containing subscripts); terminal symbols (of the generative component) are of two types: lexical symbols are written with small initial letters (they are not used in our sample, but see Section 6.2), the functors such as *R* with a subscript (the third type of semantemes, i.e., the suffixes, are rendered as subscripts). "Rule" (d) is a schema abbreviating two rules concerning coordination, which is treated here—for the purpose of the present considerations—only in a rudimentary form; for a more adequate description of coordination in the generative component, see Section 4.1.1.
5. R_a is a functor interpreted as the relation of actor to action; here the notion of actor also includes the so-called bearer of action or of quality; it is, of course, possible that a more detailed elaboration will show it useful to distinguish more units with distinct syntactic properties; cf. Section 2.1.3. A functor can be read as a functor of two arguments in a calculus with Polish notation, standing to the right of its arguments.
6. But the relation of a question to a declarative proposition of the form *I request that you tell me wh-* . . . is considered here as a coincidence of content only, not as an identity of meaning, the tectogrammatical (or "deep") structure of two such propositions being different in a crucial point: in one of them the interrogative modality as a grammatical feature is present, in the other it is not (the same content is conveyed here by lexical means).

7. According to Kopečný, some interjections should also be classed as sentences, not merely as sentential equivalents (since they are synonymous with imperatives, etc.), while some can be used in the position of a predicate verb. These questions, as well as the problems raised by infinitive sentences, are left out in our discussion, since they primarily concern the relation between different levels; their solution is necessary for a detailed formulation of the transductive components.
8. Even so we leave aside some more complicated cases; see Section 2.2.3.
9. If both variants of the order are present, we include in the list of rules (cf. Section 6.2) the one that corresponds to the basic (unmarked) variant, insofar as this variant can be determined in a simple way.
10. With the exception of the case in which the transitive verb is used "absolutely," which is possible only with certain transitive verbs (see for instance Daneš, 1964a, p. 232); in our set of rules (Section 6.2), see especially Rules 10 and 12 to 14.
11. A systematic investigation of the relationship between a coordinated (or plural) subject (with reciprocal reflexive construction) and the construction containing *s někým* (*with someone*) will be necessary. As to the possibility of distinguishing between different types of goal, see Section 2.1.3.
12. The compound predicate contains either a main verb with a verb such as *to begin*, *to continue*, a modal verb, or a copula with a noun phrase or an adjective.
13. In the Czech sentence, there is no equivalent of the English *as*, that is, *sportovec* is a predicate noun; the adjective is usually considered its attributive.
14. Here "function" refers to a unit of the given level (included explicitly in the representation of the sentence on this level), whereas "form" refers to a unit of the next lower level; "word" is used for "word-form token"; cf. the specification of word and word-form for various levels, Section 2.1.3.

4. SOME OPEN QUESTIONS

4.1 QUESTIONS OF SYNTAX

4.1.1 COORDINATION

A conjunction chain of the type $A+B+ \ldots +N$ cannot be assigned an adequate structural description, namely a description not imposing too much structure, by means of any phrase-structure grammar. This was one of the arguments of Chomsky, Lees and others in favor of transformational grammar. But it is known now that even a transformational description cannot face this problem without requiring an infinite number of rules (or of initial strings), since its way of constructing the structural description is too closely related to the derivational and transformational history of the sentence, so that there is again the information involved whether A and B or, say, B and C were connected "sooner" by an application of a transformational rule (see Pitha, 1966, for a more precise statement of the difficulties briefly sketched here). But a system using only the terminal strings of each component as members of the structural description of a sentence (and working with complex symbols) can account for the distinction between a coordination chain and a hierarchy as $((A+B)+(C+D))$—for example *John and Jane and Peter and Mary are walking in the garden*. In the generative component of a description of the type proposed here, rule schemata (i), (ii), (iii) can be inserted:

(i) $Y \longrightarrow (Y\ Y_i)$ where Y stands for *Enunc*, *Interr*, or *Voc*, and i stands for any kind of coordinative conjunction, for example for *copul*, *grad*, *disj*, *adv*, *cont* (realized in English by *and*, *and even*, *or*, *but*, *whereas*, respectively) etc.

(ii) $Y_j \longrightarrow Y\ Y_j$ where j stands for any kind of conjunction that can be connected into chains —that is, for *copul*, *disj*.

(iii) $Y_i \longrightarrow Q_i\ Y$

Applying rules (i) and (iii) cyclically, one gets (an indefinitely deep hierarchy of) simple coordination phrases, whereas applying (ii) after (i) one gets a chain, etc.

But other questions remain open. They concern, in the first place, the transductive components, which should be so formulated that

(a) a sentence such as *Rome was founded by Romulus and Remus* is described as a paraphrase of *Rome was founded by Romulus together with Remus*, not as a coordination of two sentences (i.e. in its tectogrammatical representation no coordination would occur); strictly speaking, the sentence is ambiguous, since it is a matter of factual knowledge that Rome was not founded once by Romulus and another time by Remus;

(b) a sentence such as *My aunt and uncle departed yesterday* would have a tectogrammatical representation showing that both the words *aunt* and *uncle* govern (a syntagm containing) the pronoun *my;*

(c) it must be granted that any tectogrammatical representation derived from a string of the form ($Y\ Q_i\ Y$) can be reduced if it satisfies special conditions (so that one of two occurrences of the same syntagm is deleted), for example in Czech *Dnešní i včerejší noviny přišly a leží na stole* (*Today's and yesterday's newspapers have come and are lying on the table*) is equivalent to a coordination of four sentences: *Dnešní noviny přišly. Dnešní noviny leží na stole. Včerejší noviny přišly. Včerejši noviny leží na stole.* (*Today's newspapers have come. Today's newspapers are lying on the table. Yesterday's newspapers have come. Yesterday*'s *newspapers are lying on the table.*), not only of two of them; a proposition conjoining only the first of them with the fourth (or the second with the third) cannot be reduced in a similar way;

(d) phenomena of concord have to be described adequately on the morphemic level (for some problems concerning Czech, cf. Sgall, 1967a, Section IV. 1.B).

The examples of transductive components given in this book do not include a description of coordination (and, therefore, we have not included rule schemata (i), (ii), (iii) in the generative component of our example); nevertheless, there are some indications of how points (a) to (d) could be accounted for (see Pit̆ha and Sgall, in prep.)

4.1.2 PHRASE STRUCTURE, CLOSENESS OF SYNTACTIC RELATION, AND WORD ORDER

Word order and intonation correspond in a certain sense to the relative closeness of syntactic relations inside a sentence (see Notes 1 and 3 to Chapter 2; and especially Section 2.2.3). This correspondence cannot be described adequately by means of the relation of realization, if a phrase-structure grammar is to be used as the generative component of the description, and if the phenogrammatical representation of a sentence models its dependency structure only, and not the relative closeness of the individual syntagms. Under such conditions it would probably be impossible to formulate the description to specify all and only the acceptable orders of the words of every Czech sentence without many quite *ad hoc* rules; our example of the generative component cannot generate, for instance, strings of the shape *Goal–Adverbial–Actor–Verb*, since the pair *Goal–Verb* is regarded as a constituent (*VP*) of the phrase *Actor–VP*, etc. Perhaps it would be possible to formulate the transductive components to change the word order in the desired manner, but there would then be a sharp distinction between sentences with different word orders on different levels, and those for which the word order remains the same. This distinction has to correspond to the distinction of primary and secondary word order (in connection with functional sentence perspective; cf. Section 4.2.1), but here it would be forced by the formalism itself, or, strictly speaking, by the phrase structure assigned to the proposition. Since the opposition of primary and secondary word order has not yet been studied at all systematically, one can scarcely say more on these questions without an empirical investigation of copious material.

At least the following questions have to be solved:

(a) Is there a semantically relevant distinction in cases such as Kuryłowicz's (1948) example *les anciens—remparts de la ville* and *les anciens remparts—de la ville?*—Kuryłowicz states that there is no grammatical distinction, but that there may be one "*du domaine de l'expression*"; cf. also Quine's (1960, p. 138) semantic analysis of the phrases *a big European butterfly* and *a European big butterfly*, and, for Czech, Šmilauer (1947, pp. 190f, 195; 1957, p. 21), as well as Hausenblas (1958, pp. 36f).

(b) Can this relevance of the closeness of syntactic relation be accounted for in terms of Firbas's "communicative dynamism" (cf. Firbas, 1961, 1962, 1964)?

(c) What are the means of realization of this distinction, if semantically relevant, and how should they be adequately described?

(d) Is there an intrinsic relation between this distinction and the word order, a relation that should be treated by the general linguistic theory?

4.1.3 RULE SCHEMATA, COMPLEX SYMBOLS, AND LOSS OF GENERALITY

In all components of the description we work with rule schemata and conventions that can be viewed as mere matters of notation, or as intrinsic features of the system (cf. Chomsky, 1965, pp. 42–45 and 75ff). In the first case the system is not adequate, because many relevant generalizations are missed; in the other case, the conventions have to be stated in the general theory dealing with descriptions of the given kind.

Before a serious attempt to formulate a general linguistic theory based on systems of the proposed type is made, the conventions can be understood only as empirical hypotheses indicating what ought to be incorporated into the theory should we attempt to formulate it. In addition to the usual conventions concerning for example the use of braces in rule schemata, there are two problems connected with this type of description:

The use of complex symbols needs to be specified in a way ensuring that the generative component is weakly equivalent to a context-free phrase-structure grammar (cf. Section 2.2.3). This can be done, as was shown by Tiede (1966), if at most one element of any complex symbol is "independent" in the sense that it can—by some rule—be rewritten alone, while other elements of the complex symbol remain unaffected by that rule. If the generative component were formulated in this way, there would be no need for schemata with variable indices.

In the transducers, too, we use schemata with "variables"—that is, symbols standing for classes of symbols. In our examples of transducers they have only the status of notational conventions, and a corresponding theoretical formulation must still be found.

4.2 QUESTIONS OF SEMANTICS

4.2.1 FUNCTIONAL SENTENCE PERSPECTIVE

Two sentences differing solely in functional sentence perspective (the theme-rheme articulation) are not mutually interchangeable in a fluent text, in the general case; there are even cases in which such sentences differ in their cognitive content (see Sgall, 1967c, 1968). Therefore, functional sentence perspective (FSP) should be modelled by the representation of a sentence on the tectogrammatical level. Chomsky (1965) seems to conceive this perspective as a matter of surface structure alone, but we do not share this view. It is necessary to distinguish FSP itself from the means of its realization;[1] in English this distinction is not so evident as in the Slavonic languages (where the word order is only to a relatively small extent restricted by grammatical rules, its prevailing function being the realization of FSP). But in English, too, FSP has its means of realization, and rules concerning their use belong to the competence of a speaker of the language. He can say, for instance, that *You have not seen this house yet. It was built two years ago* is a (part of) fluent text, whereas *You have not seen this house yet. Two years ago it was built* is not (at least with an "unmarked" intonation). Similarly, *Tomorrow Charles is leaving for Paris* is acceptable as an answer to *What is Charles doing tomorrow?* or *Where is Charles going?* but not to *When does Charles leave?*

The properties of Czech word order (and, to a somewhat lower degree, those of Russian) permit us to regard tentatively the order of symbols on the tectogrammatical level as corresponding to the order of lexemic units with regard to their degree of "communicative dynamism" (cf. Firbas, 1961, 1962, 1964), that is to say, each lexical sememe has a higher degree of communicative dynamism than those standing to the left of it. In the unmarked cases, this order of symbols is also identical with the actual word order on the lower levels; in other cases there is some grammatical rule changing the order (and this is to be modelled by the rules of one of the transducers; see Section 2.2.5 for the restrictions that are to be checked here empirically) or some stylistic choice (e.g., Mathesius's (1961) "subjective" word order can be used in case of emphasis).

In the proposed description, the order of symbols on the tectogrammatical level can be interpreted as outlined above, but a far more detailed classification of lexical semantemes and phrases (i.e., more non-terminal symbols) would be needed if the marked and unmarked variants of different types of syntagms were to be characterized as such. Moreover, not only the scale of communicative dynamism, but also the boundaries of the theme and the rheme of the sentence should be characterized, as well as the relationships between a declarative sentence and questions to which it can be answer (cf. Staal, 1967). But it is presumably not possible to account for all this in any description having the sentence as the main unit; only in a description working with units corresponding to text (as sentence corresponds to utterance), or regarding a proposition as a unit realized by a string of sentences, could functional sentence perspective (as well as other phenomena of intersentential character) be modelled adequately.

4.2.2 MEANING AND MEANINGFULNESS

Our attention has been focussed not on lexical semantics, but on questions concerning the meaning of a sentence, as composed of its parts, that is, on the semantic characteristics of morphological units and syntactic relations. We believe this delimitation to be useful for a more thorough consideration of the semantic relation as a whole, since the articulation of this relation is more apparent here than in the vocabulary (with respect to vocabulary, linguists usually speak only about the forms and meanings of words, without any intervening levels; but when they turn to morphological units they often study such levels as morphophonemics, morphemics, and the syntactic and semantic structure of the sentence). Of course, we do not mean to claim that lexical semantics can be described fully by the means sufficient for the area discussed here, or that this or that meaning of the word "semantics" is to be preferred.

It appears to us that the whole field of semantics has to be divided into several domains or strata, that is the presystematic notion of meaning should be explained by means of several explicit notions. As is well known, there are at least three "degrees" of meaning: extensional meaning (reference, denotation), intension (designation), and the meaning as it is "coined" by the properties of language (cf. 2.1.1), including its linearity (i.e., the linear character of the text), and with it the functional sentence perspective. Only the last of these three notions can be described by purely linguistic methods. But we cannot describe it completely without having at our disposal a description of the first two; thus, for instance, a description of the use of anaphorical pronouns, the meaning of which primarily concerns reference (cf. Palek, 1967), cannot be formulated without an explication of the first of the three notions.

Furthermore, the task of semantic description of a natural language can be specified in various ways, and it is necessary to be clear about what task we have in mind. We want to point here to some of the possibilities—without claiming that the list is full and arranged in due order.

(a) Not only the set of grammatical sentences, but also that of meaningful sentences should be specified by the generative (or other) description.

(b) An effective procedure should be formulated, enabling us, given a representation of a sentence on the phonetic level, to discover the meanings of the sentence (i.e., the corresponding representations on the tectogrammatical level, or even on a higher level), and an "inverse procedure," assigning to every description of the meaning of a sentence all the sentences having this meaning and only them.

(c) As many different descriptions of semantic structure should be assigned to each sentence as it has meanings (according to the speaker's intuition).

(d) Not only the semantic structure of the sentence, but also the semantic structure of the word, more precisely, of the naming unit, including the phraseological idiom, should be described formally.

The available empirical knowledge of semantic questions and the theoretical approaches to semantics so far formulated cannot, in our opinion, serve as the starting point for an explanation of all these matters jointly by means of a single formal system. Some of these tasks are more remote than others from the possibilities—and the actual needs—of contemporary linguistics.

As to point (a), it is not certain whether the vague notion of meaningfulness can form a sound basis for linguistic explanation. It is probably impossible to draw a boundary between meaningful and meaningless sentences using only linguistic criteria without external factual information: if, as has been said, cannibalism is not to be excluded as ungrammatical, then it should not be excluded as meaningless either. Some decades ago expressions referring to bringing a stone from the moon, or to a conversation between machines (and not to the impossibility of such things), were meaningless to the same degree as, for instance, those mentioning clever chairs or the weight of conscience. Perhaps a change of the corresponding linguistic units can be stated (e.g. moon was once connected, but is no longer, with a semantic marker "inaccessible"); but are not such answers *ad hoc*, and is it really the job of linguistic description to register in such a way all discoveries changing the usual conditions of the use of words? The discussion about problems of this kind has only begun recently, and we can only hope that it will bring some generally acceptable results.

Point (b), and, in this connection, also (c) seem to be more urgent and capable of a more complete fulfillment under current conditions.[2] Note that these points are connected not only with generative (or recognition) description of language, but also with synthesis (or analysis) for automatic translation. Of course, these points are also connected with various open questions. It is not clear, for instance, what criteria should be used in judging whether two given sentences are paraphrases or not (i.e., whether their tectogrammatical representations should be identical);[3] it is especially difficult to account for pairs of sentences where a certain unit of meaning is conveyed in one sentence by a lexical item, and in the other by a grammatical unit (cf. Panevová, 1967).

As for point (d), fruitful ideas are contained especially in the work of J. J. Katz and his co-authors, but only a systematic elaboration of a comparatively large part of the lexicon of some language from their point of view could show whether it is possible to regard this approach as appropriate for the questions of lexical semantics. Until then it remains uncertain whether such semantic properties as those assigned by Katz (1966b) to the word *good*, the conversion of relations (e.g. the relationship between *A is before B* and *B is after A*), Fillmore's entailment, or the relations studied by Mel'chuk and Zholkovskij belong to the level of meaning or to that of content.

Various examples often cited as instances of the conversion of relations or of similar phenomena do not belong, probably, to the same layer. There are, on the one hand, cases such as the passive, distinctions of intonation or of word order, connected with the functional sentence perspective. On the other hand there are cases that should not be classed as paraphrases, probably, for they convey the same content only under certain circumstances; their meanings should be considered distinct. For instance the Czech sentence *prodával noviny kolemjdoucím* (which can perhaps be translated as *he was selling the newspapers to the passers-by*) is not a paraphrase of *kolemjdoucí od něho kupovali noviny* (*the passers-by were buying the newspapers from him*); the first sentence can be true even under such conditions, where the second is not, cf. the sentence *druhý den zase prodával noviny, ale nikdo od něho nic nekoupil* (*he was again selling the newspapers the next morning but nobody has bought anything from him*); in other words, the imperfective *prodával* denotes the process as such, only the perfective *prodal* includes in its meaning also the result of the action (cf. the Latin *imperfectum de conatu*). Having this in mind, we should not regard as paraphrases even the perfective counterparts, such as *Karel prodal noviny Pavlovi* (*Charles sold the newspapers to Paul*) and *Pavel koupil noviny od Kàrla* (*Paul bought the newspapers from Charles*), since the same cognitive content is in each of them modified by linguistic units in a different way.

But there are cases belonging to neither of these two extreme instances; Jakobson (1936, p. 251) compares the Russian sentences *Latvija sosedit s Estonijej* (*Latvia neighbors on Estonia*) and *Estonija sosedit s Latvijej* (*Estonia neighbors on Latvia*). Following Husserl's treatment of pairs such as *larger than—smaller than*, he says that the meanings of the two members of such a pair are not identical, since they differ in the "Held der Darstellung, von dem ausgesagt wird." The last words lead to an assumption that even here the distinction is that of theme ("das, wovon ausgesagt wird") and rheme. In this case, of course, *Latvija sosedit s Estonijej* would be a paraphrase of *S Latvijej sosedit Estonija* (*It is Estonia that neighbors on Latvia*). The distinction between *Latvija sosedit s Estonijej* and *Estonija sosedit s Latvijej* has something in common with the distinction between *It was built two years ago* and *Two years ago it was built* in Section 4.2.1, differing from the later one in that with *sosedit* both variants have an unmarked word-order (not influenced by their contexts; see Firbas, 1962, 1964 and Sgall, 1968), while in the example from Section 4.2.1 word-order of the second variant is restricted to certain contexts (this consideration we owe to Prof. Dokulil).

In a sense, then, there is a similar relation between these two pairs, as between *mít* (*to have*), *patřit* (*to belong*) and active—passive of other verbs, or between *spát* (*to sleep*)—*bdít* (*to wake*) and negation. It is possible, in the description of a language, to characterize *bdít* as a variant of *nespat* (i.e., of the negation of *spát*), or *patřit* as an "idiomatic" passive of *mít* (in some of its meanings, etc.). But, as Bar-Hillel (1967) has shown, the typical cases of conversion of relations have to be described by other than lexical means. It is an open question whether this can be done within the framework proposed here (perhaps with inclusion of another level, "higher" than tectogrammatics, or with other changes).

4.3 CONCLUDING CONSIDERATIONS

4.3.1 A TRANSFORMATIONAL OR TAXONOMIC DESCRIPTION?

The term "transformational" is used by Chomsky and his followers in two distinct meanings; in the first a transformational description (grammar, component) is characterized by a certain form of rules (differing from rewrite rules in that they do not merely change one string into another, but affect whole P-markers; cf. Chomsky, 1955, 1957, 1961, etc.); in the second sense the term "transformational" is opposed to "taxonomic" with respect to the strong generative power of the description (cf. esp. Chomsky, 1965, pp. 88–90, where it is stated that grammars of a certain kind, if they use complex symbols, are to be classed as transformational grammars, even if their weak power is not greater than that of phrase-structure grammars). It can be seen that in this sense our description, using complex symbols and functors (equivalent in a sense to the labelled brackets mentioned by Chomsky), should be considered non-taxonomic, even though it does not use transformational rules.

Furthermore, our description does not share one of the main disadvantages of taxonomic descriptions (cf. Chomsky 1962a), namely the symbols rewritten and transformed during the generation and transduction of a sentence may bear no very direct relation to any of the subparts of this sentence; cf. Section 2.2.5 above. This point can be illustrated by the well-known examples cited so often as arguments favoring transformational description as against phrase-structure grammar:

(a) In transformational description, syntactic relations are distinguished that cannot be kept apart in any taxonomic description assigning to a (non-ambiguous) sentence only a single syntactic structure; cf. *the shooting of the hunters*. In a description of the type proposed here, this construction is considered homonymous on the phenogrammatical level, but there are two distinct tectogrammatical representations (both realized by the phrase cited):

(i) *shoot hunters* R'_a

(ii) *shoot hunters* R'_g

(we give here the orthographic forms instead of the tectogrammatical units); if nominalized, both these representations are changed to the phenogrammatical representation corresponding to the string cited above.

(b) The transformational description reflects the close relationships of some sentences for which the taxonomic descriptions are quite distinct but where close similarity is acknowledged by the speaker's intuition as well as by traditional linguistics (e.g. a statement and a corresponding question, or a subordinate clause and a corresponding nominalization). Supposing the structures of such sentences to differ in a single point, we then have to say whether this distinction has a semantic bearing or not. In the former case this distinction has to be reflected in the tectogrammatical representation of such sentences; for instance, the distinction between statement and question is accounted for by the symbol of sentence modality. In the derivation of two such propositions the distinction originates in the different choice of the symbol rewriting the symbol *Proposition* (cf. Section 6.2); this is the formal equivalent of the statement that two such strings differ just as two types of sentences (since *Proposition* is the symbol from which tectogrammatical representations of sentences are derived), and not as, say, two types of predication or of verbal phrase. In the latter case, where the distinction is not semantically relevant, we have two synonymous sentences; their tectogrammatical representations are identical, and during the transduction to one of the lower levels, there is a possibility of choice among two or more alternatives (see Table 2 in Section 6.4 for the distinction between active and passive or that between subordinate clause and nominalization).

(c) Transformational description accounts for sentences in which word order does not correspond with syntactic articulation (formulated usually in terms of phrase structure), for example English questions of the type *Has John money?* where the *VP* is to be treated as discontinuous in a phrase-structure grammar. In a description of the type proposed here such grammatically conditioned word order should be accounted for by changing the order of symbols in the transduction from the tectogrammatical level (where the order of symbols would be in accordance with the syntactic articulation) to the phenogrammatical. In some cases, as with the Czech enclitical words, the actual word order would be gained only on the morphemic level (see Section 2.2.5 for the restrictions that have to be presupposed in such cases).

(d) The transformational description does not assign "too much structure" to sentences like *He is an easy fellow to please*, which cannot be described adequately by phrase-structure grammar. In the Czech language, there are similar cases, and their treatment is illustrated here by phrases of the type *větší město než Praha* (*a larger city than Prague*); see Section 3.4.

4.3.2 LINGUISTIC DESCRIPTION AND TRANSLATION

Beside the main conditions laid on generative descriptions, which we cited as (a) and (h) in Section 1.1, a third (which is not just a stronger version of the second) is sometimes formulated; this is done most clearly perhaps by Katz (1966a): an optimal linguistic description has such a form that it can be considered a description of a part of the structure of the mechanism with which the users of a language are equipped. But it is not clear if there exists now a type of description that could possibly meet this condition.

As to transformational description, where the syntactic base is a recursive device, the semantic component being interpretative, it can scarcely be considered a model of a mechanism enabling the speaker to find (by a finite number of steps) the syntactic structure of a previously chosen message (cf. Sgall, 1967b).

Nor can the type of description specified in this book be considered adequate in this sense, for at least two reasons: (1) the generative component is not suited, in the form given here, to specifying the context restrictions and the different possibilities of word order (at least not in a relatively simple manner); (2) the transductive components, consisting of pairs of pushdown automata, are not likely to provide a model of mechanisms internalized by language users. These two obstacles (especially the second) could, perhaps, be removed by a description working with graphs (projective rooted trees) instead of strings of symbols (cf. Section 2.2.2 and the literature quoted there).

If the semantic relation is the proper object of linguistics, as we argued in Section 1.3.1, then it is not necessary to use, in a linguistic description, a generative component specifying the set of messages (or propositions) in such a way that it could model the structure of a mechanism internalized by language users. Probably such an aim is not even attainable by linguistic means alone, without the aid of psychology and other sciences. Moreover, in Section 4.2.2 we came to the conclusion that among various questions concerning semantics the most urgent (and those attainable by methods now at our disposal) are those primarily concerning the transductive components of linguistic description.

But questions of transduction are also relevant to translation. Bearing in mind that the description of the complicated relationship between the tectogrammatical and the phonetic levels, and not the selection of the message (or proposition), belongs to the classical aims of linguistics, we consider our main object to be to model the part of the mechanism used by the speaker and the hearer that concerns the translator, who has to discover the meaning(s) corresponding to a certain phonetic string and *vice versa*, but not to choose the meaning itself.

Of course, it is necessary to distinguish between cases where translation proceeds simply as an operation on texts, without use of non-linguistic knowledge and knowledge obtained from the translated text itself, and cases in which the translator has to obtain from external sources information not contained in the text, but required by the grammar of the target language.[4] We are concerned here only with translation in the narrow sense, not with conditions of choice depending on external criteria.

Another remark concerns the confrontation of the tectogrammatical levels of two languages, necessarily made by a translator. An ideal case would be the full coincidence of these two levels. But we do not share the views of some linguists, according to whom there is a level (deep structure, semantic interpretation, or whatever the term may be) actually common to all languages (cf. Section 3.1). We assume that, generally, the translator has to use (if he translates correctly) some routine converting tectogrammatical representations (propositions) of one language into those of the other language. This part of the mechanism is of course not modelled by a description of a single language; but specification of these interlanguage mappings is needed, and is directly relevant not only to automatic translation, but also to general linguistic theory.

Hence we arrive at the conclusion that the connection between algebraic linguistics and automatic translation is intrinsic. This connection is of importance to practical research (where research in automatic translation, using the findings of algebraic linguistics, makes it possible to study its empirical questions and to test its working hypotheses on large masses of texts). Moreover, the relationship between the theory and the purposes of translation (and, of course, information retrieval and similar applications presupposing syntactic and semantic analysis of texts in natural language) has a bearing on the understanding of the theoretical concepts themselves. The importance of this aspect will undoubtedly increase, as theory proceeds from the study of individual languages to the specification of language universals and other types of relationship between natural languages, and to the description of language in general.

4.3.3 NECESSITY OF EMPIRICAL RESEARCH

It is well known that the generative approach makes it necessary to describe in an explicit way not only the different units of language and their relationship (in our case, first of all to specify what units realize and are realized by the given unit), but also all the context criteria relevant for the choice of the corresponding (realizing or realized) unit. In the syntax and semantics of natural languages there are, in this respect, many points in which our knowledge of the empirical facts is not yet systematized enough by grammars of the classical type (i.e., not even observational adequacy has been achieved). Consequently it cannot be maintained that all the relevant facts can be described adequately by a system with certain stated formal properties. Under these circumstances every proposed type of description is tied to an empirically unverified presupposition that no counter-examples will be found in future research. Therefore, our assumption of Section 1.3.4 remains a mere assumption. But it is perhaps advantageous to have more such proposed types of description that can be developed in detail, confronted with each other, and verified empirically, step by step. Even if further research shows that the original proposal has to be changed—either in detail or in its structure—which is most probable, we hope that it can be useful in throwing new light on known questions and bringing in new ones.

NOTES

1. The most important of them are intonation (cf. e.g. Daneš, 1960, p. 45) and word order, but there are also other means, such as articles or pronouns, constructions with *it is . . . that*, etc.
2. Their fulfillment is limited, of course, by the impossibility of giving a precise account of point (a).
3. For instance, such a pair of sentences as *There are two chairs in this room* and *Among the objects in this room two are chairs* have the same truth-value conditions, but their

meanings are not identical: the first of them speaks only about chairs, not about other objects in the room (as the second does); in technical language, a distinction of meaning (not of truth-value conditions) must be assigned to pairs of sentences each of which can be deduced from the other.

4. This latter type can be characterized by examples like *king John's son* translated to German either as *ein Sohn des Königs J.* or as *der Sohn des Königs J.*; cf. Revzin and Rozencvejg (1964, p. 62).

5. THE MATHEMATICAL FORMULATION

5.1 BASIC NOTIONS

In this part we shall describe a mathematical system that meets the conditions presented in Chapter 2 and can be interpreted as a linguistic description of the type proposed here. The system concerned is an ordered triple (G, H_1, H_2), where G is a context-free phrase-structure grammar and H_1, H_2 are two ordered pairs of pushdown-store transducers: $H_n=(\mathbf{T}_{2n\text{-}1}, \mathbf{T}_{2n})$ for $n=1, 2$, the following condition of coherence being satisfied: the language $\mathbf{L}_G$ generated by the grammar G is a subset of the input language of $\mathbf{T}_1$ and the output language of $\mathbf{T}_k$ is a subset of the input language of $\mathbf{T}_{k+1}$, $k=1, 2, 3$. (These notions will, of course, be specified in a precise way further on.) $\mathbf{L}_G$ is interpreted as the tèctogrammatical level of the description (cf. Section 2.1.2).

The set of output strings of H_1 (or H_2) that correspond to elements of $\mathbf{L}_G$ under transduction is interpreted as the phenogrammatical (or morphemic) level (but cf. Sections 2.1.4 and 2.2.5). Thus H_1 translates representations of sentences from the tectogrammatical level to the phenogrammatical and similarly H_2 translates representations of sentences from the phenogrammatical level to the morphemic.

The present Chapter is divided into four sections. The first deals with the notion of a pushdown-store transducer, the second describes the system, the third contains a general outline of the proof concerning the condition of coherence (Theorem 1; a detailed presentation of the proof can be found in Goralčíková and Nebeský, 1968) and the fourth presents the statement that the structural description of a sentence (i.e., the sequence of its representations on the tectogrammatical, phenogrammatical, and morphemic levels) uniquely determines the sequence of computations of all the transducers as they transduce this sentence from one level to the next (Theorem 2) and, finally, a proof of the existence of a recognition procedure for the system as a whole (Theorem 3).

The notion of pushdown store automaton has been elaborated in connection with its linguistic applications by Oettinger, 1961, Chomsky, 1963, and Evey, 1963. It is used here in a form similar to that of Evey (henceforth EPSM).

In an informal way, a pushdown store transducer can be regarded as a device that works with input and output tapes (each tape is divided into segments of equal size, on each of which at most one symbol can be written). The automaton has a control unit (the structure of which can be represented by means of a set of internal states), a reading head, and a writing head; each tape moves one segment in a fixed direction whenever a symbol has been read from it or written on it. The tape grows at one end, so that as it moves in one direction its end can never reach the reading (or writing) head of the automaton (since a new blank segment is spliced onto the tape). It is assumed that whenever a new symbol is written on a tape, the symbol occupying the position that is being filled is simultaneously erased. Besides the parts mentioned above, the automaton has another tape, which has two heads: a right-reading head and a left-writing head. The writing head moves the tape to the left; an arbitrary amount of information can be written on the tape, since it grows at its right-hand end. In the course of reading, the tape moves to the right; whenever a symbol is read from the tape, it is essentially erased, because the machine can never go back to reread this symbol without writing something over it. This tape serves as a storage device and is called a pushdown store. (In the sequel we use the verbs "to read" and "to write" in connection with input and output tapes respectively, while in connection with operations with the storage tape the verbs "to insert" and "to remove" are used.)

We have found it useful for our purposes to modify the form of EPSM; in some cases we replace a finite non-empty set of rules with a single rule. From this has originated the form of a "complex" pushdown store automaton (CPSM), which will be used in this work. Every EPSM is a CPSM, and every CPSM can be replaced by an EPSM in such a way that its rules are "atomized" into the form of Evey's rules, the input and output languages remaining the same and each input string being assigned the same output string by the CPSM as by the corresponding Evey automaton.

Our aim is not to develop a general theory of CPSM or even a formal theory for a rigorous confrontation of CPSM with EPSM. (Let us add that the conceptual apparatus used by Evey—esp. his notion of the equivalence of automata—cannot be used in this case.) Our aim is only to investigate the relationships among four special classes of CPSM automata; we shall introduce here only those notions about CPSM that our investigation requires. In this connection it should be noticed that our conceptual apparatus is not quite parallel with that of Evey; for example the term computation is used for a formal structure slightly different from his, though in fact the content of the term is preserved.

One remark should be added: An EPSM reads the input tape from the left to the right and writes on the output tape in the opposite direction. With our automata, the input tape is read from the right to the left and the symbols are written from the left to the right. This divergence, formally not a substantial one,[1] has its linguistic justification in our automata $\mathbf{T}_2$ and $\mathbf{T}_4$ (this allows for the interpretation of the order of symbols by means of the rule "*regens post rectum*").

We employ the following notation: θ denotes the empty set. Let $A \neq \theta$ be a set of symbols. Then A^∞ denotes the free monoid over A, that is, the set of all finite strings composed entirely of symbols in A; the identity element of A^∞ is denoted by Λ. Strings of symbols are usually denoted by small bold-face letters, for example $\mathbf{a}$, $\mathbf{a}_1$, etc. Let $\mathbf{a}, \mathbf{b} \in A^\infty$; then $\mathbf{a}\ \mathbf{b}$ denotes their concatenation; hence $\mathbf{a}=\Lambda\mathbf{a}=\mathbf{a}\Lambda$; $dl(\mathbf{a})$ denotes the length of $\mathbf{a}$. That means: if $\mathbf{a}=\Lambda$, then $dl(\mathbf{a})=0$; if for some $n>0$ there exist, $a_1, \ldots, a_n \in A$ such that $\mathbf{a}=a_1 \ldots a_n$, then $dl(\mathbf{a})=n$. Let $\mathbf{a}, \mathbf{b} \in A^{\infty}$. If there exists $\mathbf{c} \in A^{\infty}$ such that $\mathbf{c}\,\mathbf{b}=\mathbf{a}$ (or $\mathbf{b}\,\mathbf{c}=\mathbf{a}$), $\mathbf{b}$ is called the right (or left)-hand part of $\mathbf{a}$. If $B, C \subset A^{\infty}$, then BC denotes the set $\{\mathbf{b}\,\mathbf{c}$, where $\mathbf{b} \in B, \mathbf{c} \in C\}$.

DEFINITION 1. Let the sets V_1, V_2, V_0, S and P be given, V_1, V_2 and V_0 are finite non-empty sets, S is a finite non-empty set containing at least the symbol s_0, and P is a finite non-empty set of pairs of triples $((\mathbf{a}, \mathbf{b}, s), (s^*, \mathbf{b}^*, \mathbf{a}^*))$, such that $\mathbf{a}\,\mathbf{b}\,\mathbf{b}^*\,\mathbf{a}^* \neq \Lambda$; $s, s^* \in S$, $\mathbf{b}, \mathbf{b}^* \in V_2^{\infty}$; $\mathbf{a} \in V_1 \cup \{\Lambda\}$, $\mathbf{a}^* \in V_0 \cup \{\Lambda\}$. Then the ordered quintuple $\mathbf{T}=(V_1, V_2, V_0, S, P)$ is a CPSM.

The sets V_1, V_2, V_0 are called the set of input symbols, of internal symbols, and of output symbols, respectively; S is called the set of internal states, P is called the defining relation (elements of P are called rules).

DEFINITION 2. Let $\mathbf{T}=(V_1, V_2, V_0, S, P)$ be a CPSM; a computation k of $\mathbf{T}$ is a sequence of pairs $((p_1, \mathbf{e}_1), \ldots, (p_n, \mathbf{e}_n))$, $n \geqslant 1$, iff

(i) $p_i=((\mathbf{a}_i, \mathbf{b}_i, s_i), (s^*_i, \mathbf{b}^*_i, \mathbf{a}^*_i)) \in P$, $i=1, \ldots, n$;

(ii) $s_i=s_0$ iff $i=1$ and $s_i^*=s_0$ iff $i=n$.

(iii) $s_{j+1}=s^*_j$, $j=1, \ldots, n-1$;

(iv) $\mathbf{e}_1=\Lambda$;

(v) there exists $\mathbf{e}^*_j \in V_2^{\infty}$ such that

$$\mathbf{e}_j=\mathbf{e}^*_j\,\mathbf{b}_j,\ \mathbf{e}_{j+1}=\mathbf{e}^*_j\,\mathbf{b}^*_j,\ j=1, \ldots, n-1;\ \mathbf{e}^*_n=\Lambda,\ \mathbf{b}^*_n=\Lambda.$$

The string $\mathbf{a}_n \ldots \mathbf{a}_1$ ($\mathbf{a}^*_1 \ldots \mathbf{a}^*_n$) is called an input (output) string of the computation k. Each computation begins and ends in state s_0, with empty pushdown store, and passes through stages $(p_j, \mathbf{e}_j)$; the strings $\mathbf{e}_j$ are called internal strings of k.

DEFINITION 3. The input (output) language of a CPSM is the set of input (output) strings of all its computations. The internal strings of a CPSM are the internal strings of all its computations.

DEFINITION 4. A CPSM is deterministic iff for each of its input strings there is exactly one computation.

Let $\mathbf{T}=(V_1, V_2, V_o, S, P)$ be a CPSM. Then $\mathbf{T}$ may fulfill the following restrictions.

Left restriction: Let pairs $((\mathbf{a}_1, \mathbf{b}_1, s_1), (s^*_1, \mathbf{b}^*_1, \mathbf{a}^*_1))$, $((\mathbf{a}_2, \mathbf{b}_2, s_2), (s^*_2, \mathbf{b}^*_2, \mathbf{a}^*_2))$ be elements of P. If $s_1=s_2$, then

(1) $dl(\mathbf{a}_1)=dl(\mathbf{a}_2)$

(2) if $\mathbf{a}_1=\mathbf{a}_2$, and if $\mathbf{b}_1$ is a right-hand part of $\mathbf{b}_2$ or $\mathbf{b}_2$ a right-hand part of $\mathbf{b}$, then $\mathbf{b}_1=\mathbf{b}_2$.

Right restriction: Let pairs $((\mathbf{a}_1, \mathbf{b}_1, s_1), (s^*_1, \mathbf{b}^*_1, \mathbf{a}^*_1))$, $((\mathbf{a}_2, \mathbf{b}_2, s_2), (s^*_2, \mathbf{b}^*_2, \mathbf{a}^*_2))$ be elements of P. If $\mathbf{a}_1=\mathbf{a}_2$, $\mathbf{b}_1=\mathbf{b}_2$, $s_1=s_2$, then $\mathbf{a}^*_1=\mathbf{a}^*_2$, $\mathbf{b}^*_1=\mathbf{b}^*_2$, $s^*_1=s^*_2$.

THEOREM 0. If a CPSM fulfills both the left and the right restrictions, then it is deterministic.

Proof: Let $g=(((\mathbf{a}_1, \mathbf{b}_1, s_1), (s^*_1, \mathbf{b}^*_1, \mathbf{a}^*_1)), \mathbf{r}_1), \ldots, (((\mathbf{a}_m, \mathbf{b}_m, s_m), (s^*_m, \mathbf{b}^*_m, \mathbf{a}^*_m)), \mathbf{r}_m))$, $m \geqslant 1$,

$k=(((\mathbf{c}_1, \mathbf{d}_1, z_1), (z^*_1, \mathbf{d}^*_1, \mathbf{c}^*_1)), \mathbf{t}_1), \ldots, (((\mathbf{c}_n, \mathbf{d}_n, z_n), (z^*_n, \mathbf{d}^*_n, \mathbf{c}^*_n)), \mathbf{t}_n))$, $n \geqslant m$

be two computations of a CPSM $\mathbf{T}$ such that $\mathbf{a}_m \ldots \mathbf{a}_1=\mathbf{c}_n \ldots \mathbf{c}_1$.

Evidently $s_1 = s_0 = z_1$, $\mathbf{r}_1 = \mathbf{t}_1 = \mathbf{b}_1 = \mathbf{d}_1 = \Lambda$. From the left restriction we get $dl(\mathbf{a}_1) = dl(\mathbf{c}_1)$. If $\mathbf{a}_1 \neq \Lambda$, then evidently $\mathbf{a}_1 = \mathbf{c}_1$; the more so, if $\mathbf{a}_1 = \Lambda$, then $\mathbf{c}_1 = \mathbf{a}_1$. According to the right restriction, it also holds that $s^*_1 = z^*_1$, $\mathbf{b}^*_1 = \mathbf{d}^*_1$, $\mathbf{a}^*_1 = \mathbf{c}^*_1$.

Let $1 \leqslant i < m$. Let us assume that the relations $\mathbf{a}_j = \mathbf{c}_j$, $\mathbf{b}_j = \mathbf{d}_j$, $s_j = z_j$, $s^*_j = z^*_j$, $\mathbf{b}^*_j = \mathbf{d}^*_j$, $\mathbf{a}^*_j = \mathbf{c}^*_j$, $\mathbf{r}_j = \mathbf{t}_j$ have already been proved for all j, $1 \leqslant j \leqslant i$; it is to be proved for $i+1$. From $s^*_i = z^*_i$ we get $s_{i+1} = z_{i+1}$; then from the left restriction and from the fact that $\mathbf{a}_i\ \mathbf{a}_{i-1} \ldots \mathbf{a}_1 = \mathbf{c}_i\ \mathbf{c}_{i-1} \ldots \mathbf{c}_1$, we get $\mathbf{a}_{i+1} = \mathbf{c}_{i+1}$; since $\mathbf{r}_{i+1} = \mathbf{t}_{i+1}$ (from $\mathbf{r}_i = \mathbf{t}_i$, $\mathbf{b}_i = \mathbf{d}_i$, $\mathbf{b}^*_i = \mathbf{d}^*_i$), we have also $\mathbf{b}_{i+1} = \mathbf{d}_{i+1}$. Since $\mathbf{T}$ fulfills the right restriction, the following relations hold: $s^*_{i+1} = z^*_{i+1}$, $\mathbf{b}^*_{i+1} = \mathbf{d}^*_{i+1}$, $\mathbf{a}^*_{i+1} = \mathbf{c}^*_{i+1}$.

From this it follows that $s^*_m = s_0 = z^*_m$; then according to the definition of computation, $n = m$.

An example:

$\mathbf{T} = (V_1, V_2, V_o, S, P)$ where

$V_1 = \{a\} \cup \{\#\} \cup \{\phi\}$

$V_0 = \{\#\} \cup \{b\}$

$V_2 = \{+\} \cup \{A, B\}$

$S = \{s_0, 1\}$

$P = \{p_1, p_2, p_3, p_4, p_5,\}$, where

$p_1 = ((\#, \Lambda, s_0), (1, +, \#))$;

$p_2 = ((\phi, \Lambda, 1), (1, A, \Lambda))$;

$p_3 = ((a, A, 1), (1, \Lambda, \Lambda))$;

$p_4 = ((a, +, 1), (1, + B, \Lambda))$;

$p_5 = ((\#, +B, 1), (s_0, \Lambda, b))$.

The input language of $\mathbf{T}$ can be defined as follows: Let us have a language $\mathbf{L}$, defined by (1)–(3):

(1) $a \in \mathbf{L}$

(2) if $\mathbf{u}, \mathbf{v} \in \mathbf{L}$, then $\mathbf{u}\,\mathbf{v}\,\phi \in \mathbf{L}$

(3) $\mathbf{L}$ contains no other elements.

Then the set $\{\#\ \mathbf{a}\ \#$, where $\mathbf{a} \in \mathbf{L}\}$ is the input language of $\mathbf{T}$. One of the possible computations of $\mathbf{T}$ is:

$k = ((p_1, \Lambda), (p_2, +), (p_2, + A), (p_3, + A\ A), (p_2, + A), (p_3, + A\ A), (p_3, + A),$ $(p_4, +), (p_5, + B))$. The string $\#\ a\ a\ a\ \phi\ a\ \phi\ \phi\ \#$ is the input of this computation, and $\#\ b\ \#$ its output.

5.2 THE FORM OF THE DESCRIPTION

We assume that finite non-empty sets $A_0, F_0, \ldots, A_4, F_4$ are given such that $A_0 \subset A_1 \subset A_2 \subset A_3 \subset A_4$ and $F_1 = F_2 = F_3 = F_4 = \{\phi\}$.

The sets $\{f' | f \in F_0\}$, $\{\tilde{f} | f \in F_0\}$, $\{\tilde{f}' | f \in F_0\}$, $\{\phi'\}$, are denoted by F'_0, $\tilde{F}_0$, $\tilde{F}'_0$, $F'_2 = F'_4$ respectively. The sets $\{a' | a \in A_{2k-1}\}$ are denoted by A'_{2k-1}, $k = 1, 2$; $A_4 \cap (F_0 \cup F'_0 \cup \tilde{F}_0 \cup \tilde{F}_0 \cup \{\phi, \phi'\}) = \theta$.

For $i = 0, \ldots, 4$ elements of the sets A_i and A'_i are called terms (unprimed and primed, respectively); elements of the sets F_i and F'_i are called functors;

(unprimed and primed, respectively); elements of the sets $\tilde{F}_i$ and $\tilde{F}'_i$ are called functors with a tilde.

Furthermore there are given: a finite set V_N, disjoint with the preceding ones and containing the element *Proposition;* a finite non-empty set $\mathbf{R}$ of ordered pairs such that: if $(w, \mathbf{a}) \in \mathbf{R}$ then $w \in V_N$ and either $\mathbf{a} \in (V_N \cup A_0)^\infty$ or $\mathbf{a} = \mathbf{b}\,\mathbf{c}\,f$ or $\mathbf{b}\,\mathbf{c}\,f'$ where $\mathbf{b}, \mathbf{c} \in (V_N \cup A_0)^\infty, f \in F_0, f' \in F'_0$; a mapping $\mathbf{t}_1$: $A_1 \times F_0 \times A_1 \rightarrow A_1$, a mapping $\mathbf{q}_1$: $F_0 \times A_1 \rightarrow A_1$, a mapping $\tilde{\mathbf{t}}_3$: $A_3 \times A_3 \rightarrow A_3$, a mapping $\mathbf{t}_{2k}$: $A_{2k} \times A_{2k} \rightarrow \mathbf{D}_k$, where $\mathbf{D}_k$ is the set of all subsets of A_{2k} and $k=1, 2$.

For purely technical reasons a mapping $\mathbf{t}_3$ is introduced: $A_3 \times \{\phi\} \times A_3 \rightarrow A_3$ such that $\mathbf{t}_3\,(a, \phi, b) = \tilde{\mathbf{t}}_3\,(a, b)$ for every $a, b \in A_3$; the same is true of the mapping $\mathbf{q}_3$: $\{\phi\} \times A_3 \rightarrow A_3$ such that $\mathbf{q}_3\,(\phi, a) = a$ for every $a \in A_3$.

The mappings $\mathbf{t}_i$ $(i=1, \ldots, 4)$ are interpreted as alterations of a certain type; if $\mathbf{t}_{2k-1}\,(a, u, b) = c$ or $\mathbf{t}_{2k}\,(a_1, b_1) = c_1$ for $k=1, 2$, then c or c_1 is interpreted as the result of the alteration of b according to a and u or that of b_1 according to a_1.

The symbol G denotes a context-free phrase structure grammar; its set of terminal symbols is $A_0 \cup F_0 \cup F'_0 \cup \{\#\}$ and its non-terminal set is V_N; its rule set is $\mathbf{R}$, its boundary symbol #, and its initial string # *Proposition* #. If $(\mathbf{u}, \mathbf{a}) \in \mathbf{R}$, then instead of $(\mathbf{u}, \mathbf{a})$ we sometimes write $\mathbf{u} \rightarrow \mathbf{a}$, as is usual in the works on generative grammars; also the symbol $\underset{\rightarrow}{\rightarrow}$ and the term *derivation* are used in accordance with Chomsky's definitions.

${}^N\mathbf{L}_G$ denotes the set of all $\mathbf{a}$ such that # $\mathbf{a}$ # can be derived by the grammar G from the string # *Proposition* #; $\mathbf{L}_G$ denotes the set ${}^N\mathbf{L}_G \cap \cap (A_0 \cup F_0 \cup F'_0)^\infty$.

The most important notions are, of course, the four CPSMs $\mathbf{T}_{2k-1}$, $\mathbf{T}_{2k}$, where $k=1, 2$. As will be shown later on, $\mathbf{T}_{2k-1}$ are deterministic (but $\mathbf{T}_{2k}$ are not).

We need the following conventions. The rules of automata are written in the form of tables; if $((\mathbf{a}, \mathbf{b}, s), (s^*, \mathbf{b}^*, \mathbf{a}^*))$ is a rule of an automaton, then $\mathbf{a}, \mathbf{b}, s, s^*, \mathbf{b}^*, \mathbf{a}^*$ are written in columns labeled I (input), RPS (read from pushdown store), IS (input state), OS (output state), WPS (write in pushdown store), O (output), respectively; further, if $n \geqslant 1$ and $\mathbf{b} = b_1 \ldots b_n$ $(\mathbf{b}^* = \mathbf{b}_1{}^* \ldots b^*{}_n)$,

then $\mathbf{b}$ $(\mathbf{b}^*)$ is written as $\begin{matrix} b_n \\ \cdot \\ \cdot \\ \cdot \\ b_1 \end{matrix} \quad \begin{pmatrix} b^*{}_n \\ \cdot \\ \cdot \\ \cdot \\ b^*{}_1 \end{pmatrix}$.

SPECIFICATION OF $\mathbf{T}_{2k-1}$, $k=1, 2$

$\mathbf{T}_{2k-1} = (V_1, V_2, V_0, S, P)$, where

$V_1 = A_{2k-2} \cup F_{2k-2} \cup F'_{2k-2} \cup \{\#\}$

$V_2 = A_{2k-1} \cup F_{2k-2} \cup F'_{2k-2} \cup \tilde{F}_{2k-2} \cup \tilde{F}'_{2k-2} \cup \{+\}$

$V_0 = A_{2k-1} \cup A'_{2k-1} \cup \{\phi\}$
$S = \{s_0, 1, 2\}$
P is defined by the following table, in which $a_1 \in A_{2k-2}, a_2, \ldots,$ $a_8 \in A_{2k-1}, f_1, \ldots, f_6 \in F_{2k-2}$.

THE DEFINING RELATION OF $\mathbf{T}_{2k-1}$

No	I	RPS	IS	OS	WPS	O
1.	#	Λ	s_0	1	+	#
2.	f_1	Λ	1	1	f_1	Λ
3.	f'_2	Λ	1	1	f'_2	ϕ
4.	a_1	Λ	1	2	a_1	Λ
5.	Λ	a_2 f_3	2	1	a_2 $\tilde{f}_3$	ϕ
6.	Λ	a_3 f'_4	2	1	a_3 $\tilde{f}'_4$	α' (see Note 2)
7.	Λ	a_4 a_5 $\tilde{f}_5$	2	2	$\mathbf{t}_{2k-1}(a_4, f_5, a_5)$	$\mathbf{q}_{2k-1}(f_5, a_4)$
8.	Λ	a_6 a_7 $\tilde{f}'_6$	2	2	$\mathbf{t}_{2k-1}(a_7, f_6, a_6)$	Λ
9.	Λ	a_8 +	2	3	Λ	a_8
10.	#	Λ	3	s_0	Λ	#

Note 1. We refer to the lines of this table as rules, although it would be more precise to call them rule schemata. (Only lines 1 and 10 are single rules; the rest are sets of rules; thus e.g. line 9 represents a set of rules for every $a_8 \in A_{2k-1}$.)

Note 2. $\alpha = \mathbf{q}_{2k-1}(f_4, a_3)$.

SPECIFICATION OF $\mathbf{T}_{2k}$, $k=1, 2$

$\mathbf{T}_{2k} = (V_1, V_2, V_0, S, P)$, where
$V_1 = A_{2k-1} \cup A'_{2k-1} \cup \{\phi\}$
$V_2 = A_{2k} \cup A^{\ominus}_{2k} \cup A^{\emptyset}_{2k} \cup \{\mathrm{O}\} \cup \{+\}$, where
$A^{\ominus}_{2k} = \{\ominus_a \mid a \in A_{2k}\}$, $A^{\emptyset}_{2k} = \{\emptyset_a \mid a \in A_{2k}\}$;
the elements of $A^{\ominus}_{2k}$ and $A^{\emptyset}_{2k}$ are called $\ominus$-terms and $\emptyset$-terms, respectively;
$V_0 = A_{2k} \cup \{\phi, \phi'\}$
$S = \{s_0, 1, 2, 3, 4\}$
P is defined by the following table, in which $a_1, a_3, a_4, a_{16}, a_{18}, a_{29} \in A_{2k-1}$, $a_2, a_5, a_6, \ldots, a_{15}, a_{17}, a_{19}, \ldots, a_{28} \in A_{2k}$, $b_1 \in \mathbf{t}_{2k}(a_2, a_1)$, $b_2 \in \mathbf{t}_{2k}(a_9, a_8)$, $b_3 \in \mathbf{t}_{2k}(a_{12}, a_{11})$, $b_4 \in \mathbf{t}_{2k}(a_{15}, a_{14})$, $b_5 \in \mathbf{t}_{2k}(a_{17}, a_{16})$, $b_6 \in \mathbf{t}_{2k}(a_{19}, a_{18})$.

THE DEFINING RELATION OF $\mathbf{T}_{2k}$

No	I	RPS	IS	OS	WPS	O
1.	#	Λ	s_0	1	+	#
2.	a_1	a_2	1	1	b_1 a_2	Λ
3.	a_3	+	1	1	a_3 +	Λ
4.	a'_4	a_5	1	2	a_4 a_5	a_5
5.	Λ	a_6 a_7 O	2	2	a_6 a_7	ϕ
6.	Λ	a_8 a_9 +	2	1	b_2 $\varnothing_{a_9}$ +	Λ
7.	Λ	a_{11} a_{12} a_{10}	2	1	b_3 $\varnothing_{a_{12}}$ a_{10}	Λ
8.	Λ	a_{14} a_{15} $\varnothing_{a_{13}}$	2	1	b_4 $\varnothing_{a_{15}}$ $\varnothing_{a_{13}}$	Λ
9.	a'_{16}	$\ominus_{a_{17}}$	1	1	b_5 $\varnothing_{a_{17}}$	Λ
10.	a_{18}	$\ominus_{a_{19}}$	1	1	b_6 $\varnothing_{a_{19}}$	Λ
11.	ϕ	a_{20}	1	3	Λ	a_{20}
12.	Λ	O	3	3	Λ	ϕ
13.	Λ	a_{21}	3	1	a_{21} O	Λ
14.	Λ	$\varnothing_{a_{22}}$	3	1	$\ominus_{a_{22}}$	ϕ'
15.	ϕ	$\ominus_{a_{23}}$ a_{24}	1	1	a_{24} O	Λ
16.	ϕ	$\ominus_{a_{25}}$ $\varnothing_{a_{26}}$	1	1	$\ominus_{a_{26}}$	ϕ'
17.	#	a_{27}	1	4	Λ	a_{27}
18.	Λ	O	4	4	Λ	ϕ
19.	Λ	+	4	s_0	Λ	#
20.	#	$\ominus a_{28}$ +	1	s_0	Λ	#
21.	a'_{29}	+	1	1	a_{29} +	Λ

The note added to the table of $\mathbf{T}_{2k-1}$ applies in this case, too.

Let $k=1, \ldots, 4$. The symbol ${}^{i}\mathbf{L}_k$ (or ${}^{0}\mathbf{L}_k$) denotes the set of all **a** such that # **a** # is an input (or output) string of $\mathbf{T}_k$.

As has been stated, the automata $\mathbf{T}_{2k}$ ($k=1, 2$) are non-deterministic; but it can be easily checked that they fulfill the left restriction. Let us now prove a lemma from which it follows that in the automata $\mathbf{T}_{2k}$ every computation is uniquely determined by its input and output.

LEMMA 0. Let $1 \leqslant m \leqslant n$ and

$g=((((\mathbf{a}_1, \mathbf{b}_1, s_1), (s^*_1, \mathbf{b}^*_1, \mathbf{a}^*_1)), \mathbf{r}_1), \ldots,$
$(((\mathbf{a}_m, \mathbf{b}_m, s_m), (s^*_m, \mathbf{b}^*_m, \mathbf{a}^*_m)), \mathbf{r}_m))$

$k=((((\mathbf{c}_1, \mathbf{d}_1, z_1), (z^*_1, \mathbf{d}^*_1, \mathbf{c}^*_1)), \mathbf{t}_1), \ldots,$
$(((\mathbf{c}_n, \mathbf{d}_n, z_n), (z^*_n, \mathbf{d}^*_n, \mathbf{c}^*_n)), \mathbf{t}_n))$

be two computations of $\mathbf{T}_{2k}$. If $g \neq k$ and $\mathbf{a}_m \ldots \mathbf{a}_1=\mathbf{c}_n \ldots \mathbf{c}_1$, then $\mathbf{a}^*_1 \ldots \mathbf{a}^*_m \neq \mathbf{c}^*_1 \ldots \mathbf{c}^*_n$, $m=n$ and if further $1 \leqslant i \leqslant m$, then

$\mathbf{a}^*_i=\phi$ iff $\mathbf{c}^*_i=\phi$
$\mathbf{a}^*_i=\phi'$ iff $\mathbf{c}^*_i=\phi'$
$\mathbf{a}^*_i=\#$ iff $\mathbf{c}^*_i=\#$
$\mathbf{a}^*_i=\Lambda$ iff $\mathbf{c}^*_i=\Lambda$

Proof. The table of the defining relation of $\mathbf{T}_{2k}$ gives a disjoint partition of the set P such that every element of the partition is formed by the rules grouped into one line in the table.

We denote by Q the set $\{A_{2k-1}, A'_{2k-1}, \{\phi\}, \{\phi'\}, \{\#\}, \{+\}, A_{2k}, \{O\}, A^{\oslash}_{2k}, A^{\ominus}_{2k}\}$, and by $\hat{Q}$ the set $A_{2k-1} \cup A'_{2k-1} \cup A_{2k} \cup A^{\oslash}_{2k} \cup A^{\ominus}_{2k} \cup \{\#, +, O, \phi, \phi'\}$. It is evident that Q is a disjoint partition on $\hat{Q}$. If $c \in \hat{Q}$, then $Q(c)$ denotes that $u \in Q$ for which $c \in u$. Let $\mathbf{c} \in \hat{Q}^{\infty}$. If $\mathbf{c}=\Lambda$, then we write $Q(\mathbf{c})=\Lambda$; if there exists $n \geqslant 1$, $c_1, \ldots, c_n \in \hat{Q}$, $\mathbf{c}=c_1 \ldots c_n$, then $Q(\mathbf{c})=Q(c_1) \ldots Q(c_n)$.

Let $\tilde{p}_1=((\tilde{\mathbf{a}}_1, \tilde{\mathbf{b}}_1, \tilde{s}_1), (\tilde{s}^*_1, \tilde{\mathbf{b}}^*_1, \tilde{\mathbf{a}}^*_1))$, $\tilde{p}_2=((\tilde{\mathbf{a}}_2, \tilde{\mathbf{b}}_2, \tilde{s}_2), (\tilde{s}^*_2, \tilde{\mathbf{b}}^*_2, \tilde{\mathbf{a}}^*_2))$ be rules from P. Then $\tilde{p}_1$, $\tilde{p}_2$ are grouped in one line of the table iff the following relations hold: $Q(\tilde{\mathbf{a}}_1)=Q(\tilde{\mathbf{a}}_2)$, $Q(\tilde{\mathbf{b}}_1)=Q(\tilde{\mathbf{b}}_2)$, $\tilde{s}_1=\tilde{s}_2$, $Q(\tilde{\mathbf{a}}^*_1)=Q(\tilde{\mathbf{a}}^*_2)$, $Q(\tilde{\mathbf{b}}^*_1)=Q(\tilde{\mathbf{b}}^*_2)$, $\tilde{s}^*_1=\tilde{s}^*_2$.

Finally, it is evident that if $((\tilde{\mathbf{a}}_1, \tilde{\mathbf{b}}_1, \tilde{s}_1), (\tilde{s}^*_1, \tilde{\mathbf{b}}^*_1, \tilde{\mathbf{a}}^*_1))$, $((\tilde{\mathbf{a}}_2, \tilde{\mathbf{b}}_2, \tilde{s}_2), (\tilde{s}^*_2, \tilde{\mathbf{b}}^*_2, \tilde{\mathbf{a}}^*_2))$ are two rules of $\mathbf{T}_{2k}$, such that $Q(\tilde{\mathbf{a}}_1)=Q(\tilde{\mathbf{a}}_2)$, $Q(\tilde{\mathbf{b}}_1)=Q(\tilde{\mathbf{b}}_2)$, $\tilde{s}_1=\tilde{s}_2$, then $\tilde{s}^*_1=\tilde{s}^*_2$, $Q(\tilde{\mathbf{a}}^*_1)=Q(\tilde{\mathbf{a}}^*_2)$, $Q(\tilde{\mathbf{b}}^*_1)=Q(\tilde{\mathbf{b}}^*_2)$ (see Rules 2, 6, 7, 8, 9, 10).

Let us now turn to the computations g and k. From what has been said above it is evident that $\mathbf{a}_i=\mathbf{c}_i$, $Q(\mathbf{b}_i)=Q(\mathbf{d}_i)$, $s_i=z_i$, $s^*_i=z^*_i$, $Q(\mathbf{b}^*_i)=Q(\mathbf{d}^*_i)$, $Q(\mathbf{r}_i)=Q(\mathbf{t}_i)$, $i=1, \ldots, m$. Since $s^*_m=s_0=z^*_m$, then $n=m$. Let the h-th step be the first in which g and k differ ($1 \leqslant h \leqslant m$). Then $\mathbf{a}_h=\mathbf{c}_h$, $\mathbf{r}_h=\mathbf{t}_h$, $s_h=z_h$. Thus also $\mathbf{b}_h=\mathbf{d}_h$ and according to what has been said, $s^*_h=z^*_h$. From Rules 1, 4, 5, and 11 to 20 we get that $h<m$ and $\mathbf{a}^*_h=\mathbf{c}^*_h$, thus $\mathbf{b}^*_h \neq \mathbf{d}^*_h$ and $\mathbf{r}_{h+1} \neq \mathbf{t}_{h+1}$. From Rules 2, 6, 7, 8, 9, and 10 it follows that there exist $b, d \in A_{2k}$, and $\mathbf{u} \in (A_{2k} \cup A^{\oslash}_{2k} \cup \{O, +\})^{\infty}$ such that $\mathbf{b}^*_h=\mathbf{u}\,b$ and $\mathbf{d}^*_h=\mathbf{u}\,d$. From Rules 2, 5, 13, 15, and 17 it follows that the symbols b and d remain in the pushdown store without any change until they are written on the output tape. From this and from Rules 4, 11, and 17 it follows that there exists some j, $h<j<m$ such that $\mathbf{a}^*_j=b \neq d=\mathbf{d}^*_j$.

From this the lemma follows immediately.

Since the proofs concerning the automata $\mathbf{T}_{2k}$ are rather complicated, we accept a certain convention, which is possible thanks to Lemma 0, just proved. Instead of $\mathbf{T}_{2k}$ we investigate a deterministic automaton (denoting it, for reasons of simplicity, by the same symbol), in which for each $b_1, b_2 \in A_{2k}$ exactly one fixed value from the set $\mathbf{t}_{2k}(b_1, b_2)$ is chosen; according to what has been said above, this value is denoted by $\mathbf{t}_{2k}(b_1, b_2)$. By virtue of Lemma 0, it is obviously sufficient for our purpose to investigate $\mathbf{T}_{2k}$, modified in the way described.

The symbol $\mathbf{L}_{2k}$, k=0, 1, 2 denotes a set defined as follows:
(1) $A_{2k} \subset \mathbf{L}_{2k}$;
(2) If $\mathbf{a}, \mathbf{b} \in \mathbf{L}_{2k}, f \in F_{2k}$, then $\mathbf{a}\,\mathbf{b}f$, $\mathbf{a}\,\mathbf{b}f' \in \mathbf{L}_{2k}$;
(3) $\mathbf{L}_{2k}$ contains no other elements.

The symbol $\mathbf{L}_{2k-1}$, k=1, 2 denotes a set defined as follows:
(1) $A_{2k-1} \subset \mathbf{L}_{2k-1}$; $A'_{2k-1} \subset \mathbf{L}_{2k-1}$;
(2) If $\mathbf{a}, \mathbf{b} \in \mathbf{L}_{2k-1}, f \in F_{2k-1}$, then $f\,\mathbf{a}\,\mathbf{b} \in \mathbf{L}_{2k-1}$;
(3) $\mathbf{L}_{2k-1}$ contains no other elements.

The symbol ${}^{N}\mathbf{L}_0$ denotes a set of strings that is obtained from the definition of the set $\mathbf{L}_0$ by the substitution of A_0 by $A_0 \cup V_N$. Languages of the type $\mathbf{L}_j$, j=0, . . . , 4, have certain well-known properties that are used in our exposition; they are illustrated by the example of the language $\mathbf{L}_1$ (or $\mathbf{L}_2$):

LEMMA 1: Let $\mathbf{a} \in (A_1 \cup A'_1 \cup \{\phi\})^{\infty}$ (or $\mathbf{a} \in (A_2 \cup \{\phi, \phi'\})^{\infty}$); iff the following two conditions hold, then $\mathbf{a} \in \mathbf{L}_1$ ($\mathbf{a} \in \mathbf{L}_2$):

(1) the number of occurrences of the elements from $A_1 \cup A'_1$ (or A_2) in the string $\mathbf{a}$ is one larger than the number of occurrences of ϕ (or ϕ, ϕ') in the same string;

(2) if $\mathbf{b}, \mathbf{c} \in (A_1 \cup A'_1 \cup \{\phi\})^{\infty}$ (or $\mathbf{b}, \mathbf{c} \in (A_2 \cup \{\phi, \phi'\})^{\infty}$), $\mathbf{b} \neq \Lambda$, are such that $\mathbf{a}=\mathbf{b}\,\mathbf{c}$ (or $\mathbf{a}=\mathbf{c}\,\mathbf{b}$), then the number of occurrences of elements from $A_1 \cup A'_1$ (or A_2) in the string $\mathbf{c}$ is equal to or less than the number of occurrences of ϕ (or ϕ and ϕ') in the same string.

LEMMA 2: Let $\mathbf{c}_1, \mathbf{c}_2 \in (A_1 \cup A'_1 \cup \{\phi\})^{\infty}$ (or $\mathbf{c}_1, \mathbf{c}_2 \in (A_2 \cup \{\phi, \phi'\})^{\infty}$), and $a, b_1, b_2 \in A_1 \cup A'_1$ (or A_2). A necessary and sufficient condition for $\mathbf{c}_1\, a\, \mathbf{c}_2 \in \mathbf{L}_1$ ($\mathbf{L}_2$) is that $\mathbf{c}_1\, \phi\, b_1\, b_2\, \mathbf{c}_2 \in \mathbf{L}_1$ (or $\mathbf{c}_1\, b_1\, b_2\, \phi\, \mathbf{c}_2$, $\mathbf{c}_1\, b_1\, b_2\, \phi'\, \mathbf{c}_2 \in \mathbf{L}_2$).

5.3 THE RELATIONSHIPS BETWEEN THE LANGUAGES $\mathbf{L}_G$, ${}^{i}\mathbf{L}_k$, AND ${}^{o}\mathbf{L}_k$

In the present section the relationships between the languages $\mathbf{L}_G$, ${}^{i}\mathbf{L}_k$, ${}^{o}\mathbf{L}_k$ and $\mathbf{L}_j$, where k=1, . . . ,4, and j=0, . . . , 4, are examined and general outlines of some proofs are given. On the basis of the definition of the languages $\mathbf{L}_G$ and $\mathbf{L}_0$ it is easy to show that $\mathbf{L}_G \subset \mathbf{L}_0$.

We now introduce two notions, which are used in the discussion of further relationships. An application of one rule will be called a step of the computation. A phase is a sequence of steps fulfilling two conditions: (1) in the first step of the phase the machine reads a symbol from the input tape; (2) the next reading (if any) in the sequence of steps of the computation falls in the first step which follows after the last step of the phase.

From the table of the defining relation of $\mathbf{T}_1$ it is clear that

(i) in the first phase of a computation the machine in state s_0 reads $\#$, inserts $+$ in the pushdown store, writes $\#$ and enters state 1 (see Rule 1); in the last phase of the computation, the machine in state 3 again reads $\#$, writes $\#$ and enters state s_0 (see Rule 10).

(ii) The sequence of intermediate phases of a computation (i.e. those that are not the first or the last) is non-empty; it is possible to read in each phase in state 1 either a functor or a term; the penultimate phase terminates in state 3, other phases (if there are any) in state 1.

If at the beginning of a phase a primed (or unprimed) functor is read, then a primed (or unprimed) functor is inserted in the pushdown store and the machine enters state 1; if an unprimed functor is read, nothing is written in this phase (see Rule 2); if a primed functor is read, then one functor is written (see Rule 3).

If at the beginning of the phase the machine reads a term, then one term is inserted in the pushdown store and the machine enters state 2 (see Rule 4). Then there are three possibilities:

(a) the phase continues by removing a term and the symbol $+$; the term is written and the machine enters state 3 (see Rule 9);

(b) the phase continues by removing a term and a primed (or unprimed) functor without a tilde; in this phase one primed (or unprimed) functor with a tilde and one term are inserted into the pushdown store; if the functor is unprimed, then one functor is written (see Rule 5), but if the functor is primed, then one primed term is written (see rule 6) and the machine enters state 1;

(c) the phase continues by removing two terms and a primed (or unprimed) functor with a tilde; if the functor was unprimed, then one term is written (see Rule 7); if the functor was primed, then nothing is written (see Rule 8); in both cases one term is inserted in the pushdown store and the machine enters state 2. Then the phase continues according to (a), (b) or (c). It is evident that the last possibility is recursive (the phase may be arbitrarily long).

In any case, however, in the intermediate phase the machine writes a string of terms (possibly empty) and then at most one functor. In the first and last phases neither a term nor a functor is written on the tape.

From the analysis of what has been removed or inserted during any phase it follows that the internal string (the content of the pushdown store) at the end of every intermediate phase has either the shape $+\,\mathbf{g}$ or the shape $+\mathbf{g}_1\, \tilde{g}_1\, b_1 \ldots \mathbf{g}_n\, \tilde{g}_n\, b_n\, \mathbf{g}_{n+1}$, where $n \geqslant 1$ and $\mathbf{g}, \mathbf{g}_1, \ldots, \mathbf{g}_{n+1}$ are strings (possibly empty) of functors without a tilde, $\tilde{g}_1, \ldots, \tilde{g}_n$ are functors with a tilde, and $b_1, \ldots, b_n$ are terms. (The internal string at the end of the last phase is empty.)

For each input term (functor) read just one term (functor) is inserted in the pushdown store (see Rule 4 (2, 3)). In any intermediate phase (except for the penultimate phase) the difference between the number of functors and the number of terms that have been removed from the pushdown store and the difference between the number of functors and the number of terms that have been inserted in the pushdown store are equal (in the case of the penultimate phase the latter difference is one less than the former): in Rules 5 and 6 a term and a functor are removed from the pushdown store and a functor and a term are inserted; in Rules 7 and 8 two terms and one functor are removed and a term is inserted in the pushdown store.

This means that at the end of every phase except the last two the difference between the number of functors hitherto read and the number of terms hitherto read equals the difference between the number of functors and the number of terms contained in the pushdown store. This difference is non-negative. At the end of the penultimate phase the latter difference is one number greater (see Rule 9); since this difference equals zero, the former difference must equal -1. Hence and from Lemma 1 it immediately follows, that if $\# \mathbf{a} \#$ is an input string of $\mathbf{T}_1$, then $\mathbf{a} \in \mathbf{L}_0$; thus ${}^i\mathbf{L}_1 \subset \mathbf{L}_0$.

As has been stated above, at most one functor is written in one phase; at the same time, either a primed functor without a tilde, or an unprimed functor with a tilde, is inserted in the pushdown store (see Rules 3 and 5). A term that is not written as the last is written at the same time when a primed functor without a tilde (see Rule 6) or an unprimed functor with a tilde is removed from the pushdown store. At any phase of a computation (except the last two) the difference between the numbers of functors and terms hitherto written equals the sum of the number of unprimed functors with a tilde and primed functors without a tilde that are in the pushdown store at the end of the given phase. Since, at the end of every phase except the last two, the content of the pushdown store has the shape $+ \mathbf{g}$ or $\mathbf{g}_1 \tilde{g}_1 b_1 \ldots \mathbf{g}_n \tilde{g}_n b_n \mathbf{g}_{n+1}$ (see above), the difference between the numbers of functors and terms hitherto written is at least zero at the end of every phase except the last two, and equals -1 at the end of the penultimate (and thus at the end of the last) phase.

However, the string written during any proper initial[2] part of any intermediate phase is a string (possibly empty) of terms. Let $\# \mathbf{x} \#$ be an output string and $\mathbf{y}$ an arbitrary proper left substring of $\mathbf{x}$. The smallest left substring of $\mathbf{x}$ that contains $\mathbf{y}$ and has been written during a complete phase is denoted by $\mathbf{z}$. If the rightmost symbol of $\mathbf{z}$ is a term, then $\mathbf{y}$ contains as many functors as $\mathbf{z}$ and less terms than $\mathbf{z}$. If the rightmost symbol of $\mathbf{z}$ is a functor, then the difference between the numbers of functors and terms in $\mathbf{z}$ is positive (see Rule 5), so that the difference between the number of functors and terms in $\mathbf{y}$ is a non-negative. This means that any proper left-hand substring of $\mathbf{x}$ contains at most as many terms as functors, and $\mathbf{x}$ contains one term more than it contains functors. Hence according to Lemma 1 it follows that if $\# \mathbf{a} \#$ is an output string of $\mathbf{T}_1$, then $\mathbf{a} \in \mathbf{L}_1$.

If the machine reads a primed functor, then in the same step it writes one functor (see Rule 3). If the machine reads an unprimed functor, then it inserts a functor in the store (see Rule 2) and later this functor is always removed and one functor is written (see Rule 5). This is the only case when a functor is written. The number of functors in an input string of a computation thus equals the number of functors in the output string. Since ${}^{i}\mathbf{L}_1 \subset \mathbf{L}_0$ and ${}^{o}\mathbf{L}_1 \subset \mathbf{L}_1$, the lengths of the input and output strings of a computation are the same.

We shall prove that if $\mathbf{a} \in \mathbf{L}_0$, then $\# \; \mathbf{a} \; \#$ is an input string of $\mathbf{T}_1$. If $dl(\mathbf{a})=1$, then $\mathbf{a}$ is a term and this case is obvious (see Rules 1, 4, 9, and 10). Let $dl(\mathbf{a})=2n+1$, $n>0$. Then according to Lemma 2 there exist a non-empty string of terms $\mathbf{u}$, a string of terms and functors $\mathbf{v}$, a term a and a functor g such that $\mathbf{a}=\mathbf{u}\, a\, g\, \mathbf{v}$ and that $\mathbf{u}\,\mathbf{v} \in \mathbf{L}_0$ is a string for which the above-mentioned assertion has already been proved. Let us denote $\mathbf{u}$ by $\mathbf{t}\, a_0$, where a_0 is a term.

If g is a primed functor, then the internal string at the end of the phase beginning with reading of the leftmost symbol of $a_0\, a\, g\, \mathbf{v}$, if $\# \; \mathbf{a} \; \#$ is read, is identical with the internal string at the end of the phase beginning with reading of the leftmost symbol of $a_0\, \mathbf{v}$, if $\# \; \mathbf{u}\, \mathbf{v} \; \#$ is read.

If g is an unprimed functor, then the internal string at the end of the phase beginning with reading of the leftmost symbol of $a_0\, a\, g\, \mathbf{v}$, if $\# \; \mathbf{a} \; \#$ is read, differs from the internal string at the end of the phase beginning with reading of the leftmost symbol of $a_0\, \mathbf{v}$, if $\# \; \mathbf{u}\, \mathbf{v} \; \#$ is read, only in the shape of one term.

Hence it follows that the phases of computation of the machine beginning with reading of the rightmost symbols from $\# \; \mathbf{t}$ are similar irrespective of whether the input string $\# \; \mathbf{a} \; \#$ or the input string $\# \; \mathbf{u}\, \mathbf{v} \; \#$ is read: they differ at most by the shape of one term in the pushdown store. The string $\# \; \mathbf{a} \; \#$ is an input string of $\mathbf{T}_1$.

From the table of the defining relation of $\mathbf{T}_2$ it is evident that

(i) in the first phase of a computation the machine in state s_0 reads $\#$, inserts $+$ in the pushdown store, writes $\#$ and enters state 1 (see Rule 1).

In the last phase of a computation the machine in state 1 reads $\#$ simultaneously with either (a) removing a term from the pushdown store, or (b) removing a $\ominus$-term and the symbol $+$ from the pushdown store.

In case (a) a term is written (see Rule 17), and the machine enters state 4; in this state the machine can continue in two ways:

(aa) the symbol $+$ is removed, the machine writes the symbol $\#$ and enters state s_0 (see Rule 19);

(ab) the symbol O (called a circle in the sequel) is removed, the machine writes an unprimed functor and enters state 4 (see Rule 18); the machine then can continue according to either (aa) or (ab).

In case (b) only $\#$ is written.

This means that in the last phase at most one term is written, followed by a string (possibly empty) of unprimed functors and the symbol $\#$.

(ii) the sequence of intermediate phases is non-empty; in state 1 it is always possible to read either a term or a functor; every intermediate phase terminates in state 1.

If a phase begins with reading of a term, then the machine can only continue in one of the following ways:

(a) a term is read at the input and simultaneously the symbol + is removed from the pushdown store; the symbol + and a term are inserted in the pushdown store, nothing is written and the machine enters state 1; this phase is the second phase, that is, the first intermediate phase (see Rule 3 or 21);

(b) a term is read at the input and simultaneously a ⊖-term is removed from the pushdown store; a ∅-term and a term are inserted, nothing is written and the machine enters state 1 (see Rule 9 and 10);

(c) an unprimed term is read at the input and simultaneously a term is removed from the pushdown store; two terms are inserted, nothing is written and the machine enters state 1 (see Rule 2);

(d) a primed term is read at the input and simultaneously a term is removed from the pushdown store; two terms are inserted, one term is written and the machine enters state 2 (see Rule 4); now the machine can continue in one of the following four ways:

(da) two terms and the symbol + are removed from the pushdown store, the symbol +, a ∅-term, and a term are inserted, nothing is written and the machine enters state 1 (see Rule 6);

(db) three terms are removed from the pushdown store, a term, a ∅-term and a term are inserted, nothing is written and the machine enters state 1 (see Rule 7);

(dc) two terms and a ∅-term are removed from the pushdown store, two ∅-terms and a term are inserted, nothing is written and the machine enters state 1 (see Rule 8);

(dd) two terms and a circle are removed from the pushdown store, two terms are inserted, one unprimed functor is written and the machine enters state 2 (see Rule 5); now the machine can only continue in one of the ways (da)–(dd).

In the course of this intermediate phase, which begins with reading of a term, nothing is written if the term read is unprimed; if the term read is primed, then a term is written followed by a string (possibly empty) of unprimed functors or nothing is written (see Rule 9).

If at the beginning of a phase the machine reads a functor, then it may continue just in the following ways:

(a) the functor in the input is read and simultaneously a ⊖-term and a term are removed from the pushdown store; a circle and a term are inserted, nothing is written and the machine enters state 1 (see Rule 15);

(b) the functor in the input is read and simultaneously a ⊖-term and a ∅-term are removed from the pushdown store; a ⊖-term is inserted, a primed functor is written and the machine enters state 1 (see Rule 16);

(c) the functor at the input is read and simultaneously a term is removed from the pushdown store; nothing is inserted, a term is written and the machine enters state 3 (see Rule 11); in this state the machine can continue in one of the following three ways:

(ca) a term is removed from the pushdown store, a circle and a term are inserted, nothing is written and the machine enters state 1 (see Rule 13);

(cb) a $\emptyset$-term is removed from the pushdown store; a $\ominus$-term is inserted, a primed functor is written and the machine enters state 1 (see Rule 14);

(cc) a circle is removed from the pushdown store; nothing is inserted, an unprimed functor is written, the machine enters state 3; then the machine can continue according to (ca)–(cc).

In the course of each phase at the beginning of which a functor is read, at most one term is written, followed by a string (possibly empty) of unprimed functors and by at most one primed functor.

From the analysis of what has been removed and inserted in the course of any phase, it follows that an internal string at the end of any intermediate phase has either the shape $+\ \mathbf{c}\ b$ or the shape $+\ \mathbf{c}\ \ominus_b$, where b is a term and $\mathbf{c}$ a string (possibly empty) of terms, $\emptyset$-terms and circles. An internal string at the beginning of the last phase has either the shape $+\ \mathbf{c}_1\ b_1$ or the shape $+\ \ominus_{b_1}$, where b_1 is a term and $\mathbf{c}_1$ is a non-empty string of circles.

It is evident that at the end of each phase at the beginning of which the machine reads a term, the pushdown store contains one symbol more than at the beginning of this phase (if only the symbols other than circles are taken into account; the number of circles, however, can change as well). If the machine at the beginning of a phase reads a functor, then at the end of the phase the pushdown store contains one symbol less (if only the symbols other than circles are taken into account).

This means that at the end of any intermediate phase the difference between the numbers of terms and functors hitherto read equals the number of symbols (other than the circles and the symbol $+$) contained in the pushdown store. It is evident that this number is always positive and at the end of the penultimate phase, that is, after the last symbol other than $\#$ has been read, it equals 1. Hence and from Lemma 1 it immediately follows that if $\#\,\mathbf{a}\,\#$ is an input string of $\mathbf{T}_2$, then $\mathbf{a} \in \mathbf{L}_1$; hence ${}^{i}\mathbf{L}_2 \subset \mathbf{L}_1$.

It is easy to see that in a phase in which a non-empty string of functors is written one circle or one $\emptyset$-term is removed from the pushdown store whenever one functor is written (see Rule 5, 12, 14, 16, and 18).

In each phase—except the last—in which a term is written (as has been stated above, in the course of a phase at most one term can be written on the tape), one $\emptyset$-term or one circle or one $\ominus$-term is inserted in the pushdown store (see Rules 4, 5, 6 (or 7, or 8), 11, 12 and 13 (or 14)).

This means that at the end of any phase—except the last—the difference between the numbers of terms and functors hitherto written equals the sum of the number of circles, $\emptyset$-terms and $\ominus$-terms contained in the pushdown store at the end of the phase. It is evident that this sum is non-zero if some symbol other than $\#$ has already been written on the tape.

The content of the pushdown store before the last phase has either the shape$+\ominus_b$ or the shape$+\mathbf{c}\,b$, where b is a term and $\mathbf{c}$ is a string of circles. In the former case the difference between the number of terms and the number of functors written before the last phase equals 1 and does not change any more. In the latter case one term and a string (length$=dl(\mathbf{c})$) of functors are written in the last phase; after the whole string has been written, the difference equals 1.

The string written in the course of any initial proper part of the intermediate phase contains at most one term and a string (possibly empty) of functors. Let $\# \mathbf{x} \#$ be an output string and let $\mathbf{y}$ be an arbitrary proper left substring of $\mathbf{x}$. The smallest left substring of $\mathbf{x}$ that contains $\mathbf{y}$ and that has been written in the sequence of complete phases is denoted by $\mathbf{z}$. Then $\mathbf{z}$ contains at least as many functors as $\mathbf{y}$, but —as has been shown above—this number is less than the number of terms it contains. Both strings contain the same number of terms. Hence it follows that $\mathbf{y}$ contains more terms than functors. Thus—according to Lemma 1—${}^{0}\mathbf{L}_2 \subset \mathbf{L}_2$.

If the machine reads an unprimed term, then in the same phase one term is inserted in the pushdown store and no symbol is written (see Rules 2, 3, and 10). If the machine reads a primed term, then either one term is removed from the pushdown store and one term is written (see Rule 4, 5, and 6 (or 7 or 8)), or one term is insertèd and no term is written (see Rule 9). This means that at the end of any phase except the last the number of terms hitherto read equals the sum of the number of terms hitherto written and the number of terms contained in the pushdown store at the end of the phase. As has already been stated, before the beginning of the last phase the internal string has either the shape $+ \mathbf{c}\, b$, where $\mathbf{c}$ is a string (possibly empty) of circles and b is a term, or the shape $+ \ominus_b$. If the internal string is $+ \mathbf{c}\, b$, then the machine has read one term more than it has written. In the course of the last phase one term is written and thus the number of terms hitherto read equals the number of terms hitherto written. If the internal string is $+ \ominus_b$, then the numbers of terms hitherto read and written are equal, and no term is written. Hence and from the fact that—as has already been stated—the output string contains one term more than functors, it follows that the lengths of the input and output strings are the same.

We shall prove now that $\mathbf{L}_1 \subset {}^{i}\mathbf{L}_2$ and hence (with respect to what has already been proved) $\mathbf{L}_1 = {}^{i}\mathbf{L}_2$.

(i) Let $\mathbf{a} \in \mathbf{L}_1$. If $dl(\mathbf{a}) = 1$, then $\mathbf{a}$ is a primed (or unprimed) term and it is evident that $\mathbf{a} \in {}^{i}\mathbf{L}_2$ (see Rules 1, 3, 17, 19, and 21).

(ii) Let $dl(\mathbf{a}) = 2n+1$, $n > 0$. Then there exist a string of functors $\mathbf{u}$, a string of terms and functors $\mathbf{v}$ and an umprimed term a such that either (A) $\mathbf{a} = \mathbf{u}\, \phi\, a\, \mathbf{v}$ or (B) $\mathbf{a} = \mathbf{u}\, \phi\, a'\, \mathbf{v}$, where $\mathbf{u}\, \mathbf{v} \in \mathbf{L}_1$ and it has already been proved that $\# \mathbf{u}\, \mathbf{v} \#$ is an input string of $\mathbf{T}_2$.

(A) Let $\mathbf{a} = \mathbf{u}\, \phi\, a\, \mathbf{v}$, then either (a) $\mathbf{u}$ is empty or (b) $\mathbf{u}$ is non-empty.

(a) If $\mathbf{u}$ is an empty string, then at the end of the phase in which the machine has read the leftmost symbol from the string $\mathbf{v}\, \#$ the content of the pushdown store (since the next phase is the last in the computation of the string $\# \mathbf{u}\, \mathbf{v} \#$) is either (aa) $= + \mathbf{c}\, b$, or (ab) $+ \ominus_b$, where $\mathbf{c}$ is a string of circles and b is a term.

(aa) If the content of the pushdown store is $+ \mathbf{c}\, b$, then by successive applications of Rules 2, 11, and 13 the machine enters state 1 and the internal string is $+ \mathbf{c}\, \mathrm{O}\, b$.

(ab) If the content of the pushdown store is $+ \ominus_b$, then it is possible to apply Rules 10, 11, and 14 in this order; the machine enters state 1, and the internal string is $+ \ominus_b$. Hence in cases (aa) and (ab) the next phase is the last phase of the computation of the string $\# \mathbf{a} \#$, and $\mathbf{a} \in {}^i\mathbf{L}_2$.

(b) If $\mathbf{u}$ is a non-empty string, then $\mathbf{u}=\mathbf{u}_1 \phi$, where $\mathbf{u}_1$ is a string (possibly empty) of functors and at the end of the phase in which the machine has read the leftmost symbol of $\mathbf{v} \#$ the content of the pushdown store is either (ba) $+ \mathbf{c}\, b$, or (bb) $+ \mathbf{c} \ominus_b$, where $\mathbf{c}$ is a string (possibly empty) of terms, $\varnothing$-terms and circles, and b is a term.

(ba) If the internal string is $+ \mathbf{c}\, b$, then by successive applications of Rules 2, 11, and 13 the machine enters state 1 and the internal string is $+ \mathbf{c} \bigcirc b$. In the next phase the machine reads a functor. Then either (baa) $\mathbf{c}=\mathbf{c}_1\, b_1\, \mathbf{c}_2$ or (bab) $\mathbf{c}=\mathbf{c}_1 \varnothing_{b_1} \mathbf{c}_2$, where $\mathbf{c}_2$ is a string (possibly empty) of circles and b_1 is a term.

(baa) If $\mathbf{c}=\mathbf{c}_1\, b_1\, \mathbf{c}_2$, then by successive applications of Rules 11, 12 and 13 the machine enters state 1 and the internal string is $+ \mathbf{c}_1 \bigcirc b_1$.

(bab) If $\mathbf{c}=\mathbf{c}_1 \varnothing_{b_1} \mathbf{c}_2$, then by successive applications of Rules 11, 12, and 14 the machine enters state 1 and the internal string has the shape $+ \mathbf{c}_1 \ominus_{b_1}$

(bb) If the internal string is $+ \mathbf{c} \ominus_b$, then by successive applications of Rules 10, 11, and 14 the machine enters state 1 and the internal string has the shape $+ \mathbf{c} \ominus_b$.

It is thus evident that in the cases (ba) and (bb) the next phases of the computation beginning with reading of the rightmost symbol from $\# \mathbf{u}_1$ are the same for the input strings $\# \mathbf{u}\, \mathbf{v} \#$ and $\# \mathbf{a} \#$. This means that $\mathbf{a} \in {}^i\mathbf{L}_2$.

(B) If $\mathbf{a}=\mathbf{u}\, \phi\, a'\, \mathbf{v}$, then either (a) $\mathbf{u}$ is empty or (b) $\mathbf{u}$ is non-empty.

(a) If $\mathbf{u}$ is an empty string, then at the end of the phase in which the machine has read the leftmost symbol of $\mathbf{v} \#$, the shape of the internal string (as has been said above in (A) (a)) is either (aa) $+ \mathbf{c}\, b$, or (ab) $+ \ominus_b$, where $\mathbf{c}$ is a string of circles and b is a term.

(aa) If the internal string is $+ \mathbf{c}\, b$, then by successive applications of Rules 4, 5, 6, 11, and 14 the machine enters state 1 and the internal string has the shape $+ \ominus_b$.

(ab) If the internal string is $+ \ominus_b$, then by successive applications of Rules 9, 11, and 15 the machine enters state 1 and the internal string has the shape $+ \ominus_b$.

In cases (aa) and (ab) the next phase will be the last phase of the computation of the string $\# \mathbf{a} \#$, and $\mathbf{a} \in {}^i\mathbf{L}_2$.

(b) If $\mathbf{u}$ is a non-empty string, then $\mathbf{u}=\mathbf{u}_1 \phi$, where $\mathbf{u}_1$ is a string (possibly empty) of functors and at the end of the phase in which the machine has read the leftmost symbol of $\mathbf{v} \#$, the internal string has one of two shapes: (ba) $+ \mathbf{c}\, b$ or (bb) $+ \mathbf{c} \ominus_b$, where $\mathbf{c}$ is a string (possibly empty) of terms, $\varnothing$-terms and circles, and b is a term.

(ba) If the internal string is $+ \mathbf{c}\, b$, then either (baa) $\mathbf{c}=\mathbf{c}_1\, b_1\, \mathbf{c}_2$, or (bab) $\mathbf{c}=\mathbf{c}_1 \varnothing_{b_1} \mathbf{c}_2$, where $\mathbf{c}_2$ is a string of circles, and b_1 is a term.

(baa) If $\mathbf{c}=\mathbf{c}_1\, b_1\, \mathbf{c}_2$, then by successive applications of Rules 4, 5, 7, 11, and

14 the machine enters state 1 and the internal string has the shape $+ \mathbf{c}_1\, b_1 \ominus_b$. In the next phase, the machine reads a functor. Then by an application of Rule 15 the machine enters state 1 and the internal string has the shape $+ \mathbf{c}_1\, \mathrm{O}\, b_1$.

(bab) If $\mathbf{c}=\mathbf{c}_1 \oslash_{b_1} \mathbf{c}_2$, then by successive applications of Rules 4, 5, and 8 the machine enters state 1 and the internal string has the shape $+ \mathbf{c}_1 \oslash_{b_1} \ominus_b$. In the next phase the machine reads a functor. Then by an application of Rule 16 the machine enters state 1 and the internal string has the shape $+\mathbf{c}_1 \ominus_{b_1}$.

It is evident that in cases (baa) and (bab) the next phases of the computations beginning with reading of the rightmost symbol from $\# \mathbf{u}_1$ are the same for the strings $\# \mathbf{a} \#$ and $\# \mathbf{u\,v} \#$. Hence $\mathbf{a} \in {}^i\mathbf{L}_2$.

(bb) If the internal string is $+ \mathbf{c} \ominus_b$, then by successive applications of Rules 9, 11, and 14 the machine enters state 1 and the internal string has the shape $+ \mathbf{c} \ominus_b$. The next phase of the computation for the strings $\# \mathbf{u\ v} \#$ and $\# \mathbf{a} \#$ is the same. Hence $\mathbf{a} \in {}^i\mathbf{L}_2$.

We have shown that $\mathbf{L}_G \subset {}^i\mathbf{L}_1$ and, furthermore, that ${}^i\mathbf{L}_1=\mathbf{L}_0$, ${}^o\mathbf{L}_1 \subset \mathbf{L}_1$, ${}^i\mathbf{L}_2=\mathbf{L}_1$, ${}^o\mathbf{L}_2 \subset \mathbf{L}_2$. It can be proved by analogous means that ${}^i\mathbf{L}_3=\mathbf{L}_2$, ${}^o\mathbf{L}_3 \subset \mathbf{L}_3$, ${}^i\mathbf{L}_4=\mathbf{L}_3$. The following theorem can be formulated:

THEOREM 1: $\mathbf{L}_G \subset {}^i\mathbf{L}_1, {}^o\mathbf{L}_1 \subset {}^i\mathbf{L}_2, {}^o\mathbf{L}_2 \subset {}^i\mathbf{L}_3, {}^o\mathbf{L}_3 \subset {}^i\mathbf{L}_4$.

Moreover, it has been stated that the lengths of input and output strings of any computation of every $\mathbf{T}_i$, $i=1, \ldots, 4$ are the same. We shall make use of this property in the next section.

5.4 STRUCTURAL DESCRIPTION AND RECOGNITION PROCEDURE

DEFINITION 5. A sequence $d=(\mathbf{a}_0, k_1, \mathbf{a}_1, \ldots, k_4, \mathbf{a}_4)$ is called a complete description iff

(i) $\mathbf{a}_i \in \mathbf{L}_i$ for $i=0, \ldots, 4$;
(ii) k_j is a computation of $\mathbf{T}_j$ for $j=1, \ldots, 4$;
(iii) $\# \mathbf{a}_n \#$ is the input of k_{n+1}; $\# \mathbf{a}_{n+1} \#$ is an output of k_{n+1}, $n=0, \ldots, 3$;
(iv) $\#$ *Proposition* $\# \overset{*}{\Rightarrow} \# \mathbf{a}_0 \#$ holds.

It may sometimes be useful to say that d is a complete description of $\mathbf{a}_4$.

An ordered triple $(\mathbf{a}_0, \mathbf{a}_2, \mathbf{a}_4)$ for which there exists a complete description $d=(\mathbf{a}_0, k_1, \mathbf{a}_1, \ldots, k_4, \mathbf{a}_n)$ is called a structural description.

THEOREM 2. For every structural description $(\mathbf{a}_0, \mathbf{a}_2, \mathbf{a}_4)$ there exists exactly one complete description $d=(\mathbf{a}_0, k_1, \mathbf{a}_1, \ldots, k_4, \mathbf{a}_4)$.

Proof. Let $d=(\mathbf{a}_0, k_1, \mathbf{a}_1, k_2, \mathbf{a}_2, k_3, \mathbf{a}_3, k_4, \mathbf{a}_4)$ and $d^*=(\mathbf{a}_0, k^*_1, \mathbf{a}^*_1, k^*_2, \mathbf{a}_2, k^*_3, \mathbf{a}^*_3, k^*_4, \mathbf{a}_4)$ be two complete descriptions. Since $\mathbf{T}_1$, $\mathbf{T}_3$ are deterministic, $k^*_1=k_1$, $\mathbf{a}^*_1=\mathbf{a}_1$, $k^*_3=k_3$, $\mathbf{a}^*_3=\mathbf{a}_3$. Then—according to the proof of Lemma 0—it also holds that $k^*_2=k_2$, $k^*_4=k_4$. Thus $d^*=d$, which was to be proved.

Notation. The set of all $\mathbf{a} \in \mathbf{L}_4$ for which there exist structural descriptions $(\mathbf{a}_0, \mathbf{a}_2, \mathbf{a})$ is denoted by $\mathbf{L}$.

THEOREM 3. Let $\mathbf{a} \in \mathbf{L}_4$. Then there exists a finite procedure that allows one to decide whether $\mathbf{a}$ is an element of $\mathbf{L}$.

Proof. If $\mathbf{a} \in \mathbf{L}$, then there must exist its complete description d. Let us suppose that it has the form $(\mathbf{a}_0, k_1, \mathbf{a}_1, \ldots, k_4, \mathbf{a})$. Then, according to the results of Section 5.3, $dl(\mathbf{a}_0) = dl(\mathbf{a}_2) = dl(\mathbf{a})$.

There is only a finite number of pairs $(\mathbf{a}_0, \mathbf{a}_2)$. It can be decided about each of them, whether $\#$ *Proposition* $\# \overset{*}{\Rightarrow} \# \mathbf{a}_0 \#$; the grammar G is context-free, so that there exists a recognition procedure for it (cf. Chomsky, 1959). Henceforth we consider only these pairs. It remains to examine whether $\mathbf{T}_1$ and $\mathbf{T}_2$ will translate $\mathbf{a}_0$ to $\mathbf{a}_2$ and whether $\mathbf{T}_3$ and $\mathbf{T}_4$ will translate $\mathbf{a}_2$ to $\mathbf{a}$. Since there is only a finite number of pairs $(\mathbf{a}_0, \mathbf{a}_2)$, $(\mathbf{a}_2, \mathbf{a})$, the finite procedure evidently exists.

Hence the theorem has been proved.

NOTES

1. A sequence of automata of our type can be replaced by a sequence of Evey's automata, but the latter must include additional simple automata "reversing" the order of symbols in the string.
2. A proper initial part of the phase $(a_1, a_2, \ldots, a_k, \ldots a_n)$ is a sequence of the shape $(a_1, a_2, \ldots, a_k)$, for $1 < k < n$.

6. A FRAGMENT OF THE DESCRIPTION OF CZECH

6.1 PRELIMINARY REMARKS

In Chapter 5 we present the basis of a formal apparatus that can be interpreted as a description of a natural language. Here we attempt a partial specification of an apparatus interpretable as a description of Czech. This specification concerns two points:

(1) Chapter 5 contains in fact only the fundamental framework of the formal apparatus, showing its main idea; even this framework has rather complicated properties. The apparatus presented in Chapter 5 solves, in a sense, the global problems of the proposed type of linguistic description. A description of a natural language, however, also requires a treatment of many more or less special questions. The present chapter advances answers to some of the questions that arise in connection with the description of Czech. For this reason, first of all, the transducers $\mathbf{T}_1$, $\mathbf{T}_2$ and $\mathbf{T}_4$ are modified (see Section 6.3) to provide for some of the types of constructions mentioned in Section 3.4: the modifications added to $\mathbf{T}_2$ allow for the deletion of the copula in constructions of the type *Adjective*+*Noun* and for the treatment of constructions such as Cz. *pět knih* (*five books*; cf. Russ. *pjat' knig*). The quite local modification of $\mathbf{T}_1$ is connected with the same task. The modification of $\mathbf{T}_4$ consists in placing each preposition or subordinate conjunction at the beginning of its phrase, and in changing the order of symbols in cases such as Cz. *větší město než Praha* (*a larger city than Prague*); $\mathbf{T}_4$ lacks the symbols ϕ and ϕ' in its output language.

The input languages of the modified transducers $\mathbf{T}_1$, $\mathbf{T}_3$, $\mathbf{T}_4$ are identical with the input languages of those in Chapter 5; strings that are elements of $\mathbf{L}_1$ and that are not contained in the input language of the modified transducer $\mathbf{T}_2$ cannot be output strings of the modified transducer $\mathbf{T}_1$ (this being insured by Rules 7 and 8 of $\mathbf{T}_1$). The output languages of both variants of $\mathbf{T}_2$ are subsets of $\mathbf{L}_2$. From this it follows that the main results of Chapter 5 are also valid for the modified transducers. A formal proof of this claim would not, of course, be simple, and it would have to be changed with every new modification of the original framework, i.e., whenever some linguistic question of a new kind is added.

(2) To specify our formal system means to specify the grammar G and the automata $\mathbf{T}_k$, $k=1, \ldots, 4$ (taking into account the modifications mentioned above). A preliminary specification of the grammar is given in Section 6.2 (but see the linguistic comments in Chapters 2 and 3). To specify the transducers means to specify the sets $A_1, \ldots, A_4$, the mappings $\mathbf{t}_1, \ldots, \mathbf{t}_4$, and the mapping $\mathbf{q}_1$. Mapping $\mathbf{t}_3$ is an identity mapping here, and mapping $\mathbf{t}_1$: $A_1 \times F_0 \times A_1 \rightarrow A_1$ can be reduced to $\mathbf{e}$, which is a mapping from $F_0 \times A_1$ into A_1.

The symbols of $A_1, \ldots, A_4$ originate by modifications of symbols of A_0. These modifications are carried out by the above-mentioned mappings and they consist in changing the original symbols or in adding new ones. These mappings account for a large number of the regularities in natural languages (restrictions on nominalization, concord, the choice of synonymous prepositions and conjunctions—insofar as it is not a matter of stylistics). We can present here (in the form of the tables of Section 6.4) only some examples showing the nature of these mappings; that is to say, only some subsets of $A_k - A_0, k \neq 0$ are given (where "$-$" means subtraction of sets).

Section 6.5 contains the derivation and transduction of a Czech sentence as an example.

6.2 SOME RULES OF THE GRAMMAR

Introductory Note. A linguistic commentary on the rules given here is presented in Sections 3.1 through 3.3; as to their formal status, see Section 5.2. The initial string is #*Proposition*#; terminal symbols are of two kinds: (a) the functors, written as R (or R') with a subscript, (b) the lexical semantemes combined with indices (interpreted as morphological semantemes). The lexical semantemes are here replaced by Czech words in their orthographical forms. Nonterminal symbols have the form of abbreviations beginning with capital letters. The concatenation of symbols is denoted by their juxtaposition. For individual rules the possible values of the index variables are specified in the notes; these variables are distinguished in that they are not printed in italics. Where variables are left without notes, they can take the values given by the last preceding relevant note. The list of rules (including rule schemata) is abbreviated by the following convention: whenever the right-hand side of a rule has the form $A\ B\ R_{\mathrm{i}}$ (where A, B are non-terminal symbols and i stands for any subscript used with a functor), a corresponding rule is implied, differing only in that its right-hand side has the form $B\ A\ R'_{\mathrm{i}}$, and *vice versa*. This convention does not apply to a rule if its left-hand side contains any of the symbols *NP*, *Nom*, *Adv*. Some of the rules could be left out (e.g. Rule 11 could be replaced by a change in the last line of Rule 10); but with them, the presentation is easier to survey.

Expansion Rules

$$1.\ \ Proposition \rightarrow \begin{cases} Declar \\ Interr \\ Voc \\ Interj \end{cases}$$

$$2.\ \ Declar \rightarrow \begin{cases} Pred_{0,\,\mathrm{0,\,asp,\,temp,\,mod,\,modal}} \\ NP_{\mathrm{modif,\,numb}} \\ Adj \\ Adv_x \end{cases}$$

where asp stands for *perf*, *imperf*, *result*, *iter;*
temp stands for *pres*, *pret*, *fut*, *gnom;*
mod stands for *ind*, *facult*, *deb*, *vol*, *possib*, *perm*, *hort;*
modal stands for *declar*, *desid*, *imper;*
modif stands for 0, 1, . . ., 68 (see the list on pp. 99);
numb stands for 0, *pl;*
x stands for 1, . . ., 10, 12

3. $Interr \rightarrow Pred_{0,\,0,\,\text{asp},\,\text{temp},\,\text{mod},\,\textit{interr}}$

4. $Voc \rightarrow N_{70,\,\text{numb}}$

5. $$Pred_{\text{modif, rel, asp, temp, mod, modal}} \rightarrow \left\{\begin{array}{l} Interj\ Pred_{\text{subscr}}\ R_v \\ Voc\ Pred_{\text{subscr},\,1}\ R_v \\ Pred_{\text{subscr},\,\text{i}} \\ VP^0{}_{\text{subscr},\,1} \\ Be_{\text{subscr},\,1}\ Adj\ R'_n \end{array}\right.$$

where modif stands for 0, 1, . . ., 69;
rel stands for 0, *simult*, *prec*, *succ;*
modal stands for 0, *declar*, *desid*, *imper*, *interr;*
i stands for 1, 2;
subscr stands for the sequence of subscripts identical with that on the left side of the rule (but see Section 4.1.3)

6. $$Pred_{\text{modif, rel, asp, temp, mod, modal, 1}} \rightarrow \left\{\begin{array}{l} NP_{0,\,\text{numb}}\ VP^0_{\text{subscr}}\ R_a \\ NP_{0,\,\text{numb}}\ PN_{\text{subscr}}\ R_a \\ NP_{0,\,\text{pl}}\ PQ_{\text{subscr}}\ R_a \end{array}\right.$$

7. $$Pred_{\text{modif, rel, asp, temp, mod, modal, 2}} \rightarrow \left\{\begin{array}{l} N_{0,\,\text{numb}}\ VP^0_{\text{subscr}}\ R_a \\ N_{0,\,\text{numb}}\ PN_{\text{subscr}}\ R_a \\ N_{0,\,\text{pl}}\ PQ_{\text{subscr}}\ R_a \end{array}\right.$$

8. $$PN_{\text{modif, rel, asp, temp, mod, modal, i}} \rightarrow \left\{\begin{array}{l} Be_{\text{subscr}}\ Adj\ R'_n \\ Be_{\text{subscr}}\ NP_{\text{modif}',\,\text{numb}}\ R'_n \\ Be_{\text{subscr}} \end{array}\right.$$

where modif′ stands for 0, 11, 20

9. $PQ_{\text{modif, rel, asp, temp, mod, modal, i}} \rightarrow Be_{\text{subscr}}\ Numer\ R'_n$

10. $$VP^0{}_{\text{modif, rel, asp, temp, mod, modal, i}} \rightarrow \left\{\begin{array}{l} V^{intrans}_{\text{subscr}} \\ V^{semitrans}_{\text{subscr}} \\ VP^1_{\text{subscr}}\ NP_{20,\,\text{numb}}\ R'_g \\ V^{loc}_{\text{subscr}}\ NP_{\text{modif}',\,\text{numb}}\ R'_m \\ V^{loc}_{\text{subscr}}\ Adv_{\text{x}}\ R'_m \\ V^{dir}_{\text{subscr}}\ NP_{\text{modif}'',\,\text{numb}}\ R'_m \\ V^{dir}_{\text{subscr}}\ Adv_{\text{y}}\ R'_m \\ V^{manner}_{\text{subscr}}\ NP_{8,\,\text{numb}}\ R'_m \\ V^{quest}_{\text{subscr}}\ Indir\ R'_g \end{array}\right.$$

where modif′ stands for 28, 32, 36, 40, 44, 48, 52, 55, 58, 61, 63, 64, ..., 68;
modif″ stands for 30, 34, 38, 42, 46, 50, 53, 56, 59, 62, 63, ..., 68;
x stands for 3, 4;
y stands for 5, 6;

11. $Indir \rightarrow Pred_{69,\ \mathrm{rel,\ asp,\ temp,\ mod,}\ 0}$

12. $VP^{j}_{\mathrm{modif,\ rel,\ asp,\ temp,\ mod,\ modal,\ i}} \rightarrow VP^{j+2}_{\mathrm{subscr}}\ NP_{0,\ \mathrm{numb}}\ R'_{g}$
where j stands for 0, 1

13. $VP^{2}_{\mathrm{modif,\ rel,\ asp,\ temp,\ mod,\ modal,\ i}} \rightarrow \begin{Bmatrix} V^{semitrans}_{\mathrm{subscr}} \\ V^{trans}_{\mathrm{subscr}} \end{Bmatrix}$

14. $VP^{3}_{\mathrm{modif,\ rel,\ asp,\ temp,\ mod,\ modal,\ i}} \rightarrow V^{compl}_{\mathrm{subscr}}$

15. $NP_{\mathrm{modif,\ numb}} \rightarrow Adv_{\mathrm{x}}\ NP_{\mathrm{subscr}}\ R_{m}$
where x stands for 13, 14
modif stands for 0, 1, ..., 68

16. $NP_{\mathrm{modif},\ 0} \rightarrow Pred_{\mathrm{modif,\ rel,\ asp,\ temp,\ mod},\ 0}$
where rel stands for *simult*, *prec*, *succ*

17. $NP_{\mathrm{modif,\ numb}} \rightarrow \begin{Bmatrix} Pron\ Nom_{\mathrm{subscr}}\ R_{m} \\ Nom_{\mathrm{subscr}} \end{Bmatrix}$

18. $Nom_{\mathrm{modif,\ numb}} \rightarrow \begin{Bmatrix} Det\ N_{\mathrm{subscr}}\ R_{m} \\ N_{\mathrm{subscr}} \end{Bmatrix}$

19. $N_{\mathrm{modif,\ numb}} \rightarrow Pred_{0,\ \mathrm{rel,\ asp,\ temp,\ mod},\ 0}\ N_{\mathrm{subscr}}\ R_{m}$
where modif stands for 0, 1, ..., 68, 70

20. $Adj \rightarrow Adject_{\mathrm{degree}}$
where degree stands for *posit*, *comp*, *sup*, *elat*

21. $Adv_{\mathrm{x}} \rightarrow Adv_{13}\ Adv_{\mathrm{x}}\ R_{m}$
where x stands for 1, ..., 9

22. $Adv_{\mathrm{x}} \rightarrow Adv_{14}\ Adv_{\mathrm{x}}\ R_{m}$
where x stands for 1, ..., 11

23. $Adv_{\mathrm{x}} \rightarrow Adv_{\mathrm{y}}\ Adverb_{\mathrm{x}}\ R_{m}$
where x stands for 3, 5, 9, 10, 12;
y stands for 8, 11

24. $Adv_{\mathrm{x}} \rightarrow Adverb_{\mathrm{x}}$
where x stands for 1, ..., 14

25. $Pred_{\mathrm{modif,\ rel,\ asp,\ temp,\ mod,\ modal}} \rightarrow \begin{Bmatrix} NP_{\mathrm{modif',\ numb}}\ Pred_{\mathrm{subscr}}\ R_{m} \\ Adv_{\mathrm{x}}\ Pred_{\mathrm{subscr}}\ R_{m} \end{Bmatrix}$
where rel stands for 0, *simult*, *prec*, *succ;*
modif stands for 0, ..., 69;
modif′ stands for 1, ..., 10, 12, ..., 19, 21, ..., 68;
x stands for 3, ..., 14

26. $Pred_{\mathrm{modif,\ rel,\ asp,\ pret,\ mod,\ modal}} \rightarrow Adv_{1}\ Pred_{\mathrm{subscr}}\ R_{m}$

27. $Pred_{\mathrm{modif,\ rel,\ asp,\ fut,\ mod,\ modal}} \rightarrow Adv_{2}\ Pred_{\mathrm{subscr}}\ R_{m}$

Selectional Rules:[1]

28. $N_{\text{modif, numb}}$ → *člověk*$_{\text{subscr}}$ (*man*), *jednotka*$_{\text{subscr}}$ (*unit*), *dávka*$_{\text{subscr}}$ (*dose*)...
29. $Adject_{\text{degree}}$ → *velký*$_{\text{degree}}$ (*large*), *obtížný*$_{\text{degree}}$ (*difficult*), *bílý*$_{\text{degree}}$ (*white*)...
30. $Pred_{\text{modif, rel, asp, temp, modal, 1}}$ → *svítá*$_{\text{subscr}}$ (*dawn*), *prší*$_{\text{subscr}}$ (*rain*), . . .
    where modif stands for 0, ..., 69;
    rel stands for 0, *simult*, *prec*, *succ*
31. $V^{intrans}_{\text{modif, rel, asp, temp, mod, modal, i}}$ → *jde* subscr (*go*), *padá*$_{\text{subscr}}$ (*fall*), ...
32. $V^{semitrans}_{\text{modif, rel, asp, temp, mod, modal, i}}$ → *píše*$_{\text{subscr}}$ (*write*), *škodí*$_{\text{subscr}}$ (*injure*), ...
33. $V^{trans}_{\text{modif, rel, asp, temp, mod, modal, i}}$ → *přináší*$_{\text{subscr}}$ (*bring*), *řeší*$_{\text{subscr}}$ (*solve*), ...
34. $V^{compl}_{\text{modif, rel, asp, temp, mod, modal, i}}$ → *volí*$_{\text{subscr}}$ (*elect*), *nazývá*$_{\text{subscr}}$ (*call*), ...
35. $V^{loc}_{\text{modif, rel, asp, temp, mod, modal, i}}$ → *octne se*$_{\text{subscr}}$ (*find o.s.in*), *usídlí se*$_{\text{subscr}}$ (*establish o.s.in*), ...
36. $V^{dir}_{\text{modif, rel, asp, temp, mod, modal, i}}$ → *směřuje*$_{\text{subscr}}$ (*aim at*), *odebírá se*$_{\text{subscr}}$ (*depart for*), ...
37. $V^{manner}_{\text{modif, rel, asp, temp, mod, modal, i}}$ → *chová se*$_{\text{subscr}}$ (*behave*), *vede si*$_{\text{subscr}}$ (*conduct o.s.*), ...
38. $V^{ques}_{\text{modif, rel, asp, temp, mod, modal, i}}$ → *zjišťuje*$_{\text{subscr}}$ (*find out*), *zkoumá*$_{\text{subscr}}$ (*investigate*), ...
39. $Be_{\text{modif, rel, asp, temp, mod, modal, i}}$ → *je*$_{\text{subscr}}$ (*be*)
40. Adverb_1 → *včera* (*yesterday*), *loni* (*last year*), ...
41. Adverb_2 → *zítra* (*tomorrow*), *napřesrok* (*next year*), ...
42. $Adverb_3$ → *dole* (*at the botttom*), *vpředu* (*in front*), ...
43. $Adverb_4$ → *venku* (*outside*), *uvnitř* (*inside*), ...
44. $Adverb_5$ → *dolů* (*downwards*), *dopředu* (*forwards*), ...
45. $Adverb_6$ → *ven* (*out*), *dovnitř* (*in*), ...
46. $Adverb_7$ → *teď* (*now*), *dnes* (*today*), *zdola* (*from below*), *spodem* (*by the low way*), *dvakrát* (*twice*), ...
47. $Adverb_8$ → *dost* (*enough*)
48. $Adverb_9$ → *schválně* (*on purpose*), ...
49. $Adverb_{10}$ → *dlouho* (*for a long time*), *často* (*often*), *silně* (*strongly*), ...
50. $Adverb_{11}$ → *hodně* (*very*), *trochu* (*a little*), ...
51. $Adverb_{12}$ → *brzy* (*soon*), *pozdě* (*late*), ...
52. $Adverb_{13}$ → *právě* (*just*)
53. $Adverb_{14}$ → *jen* (*only*)
54. *Interj* → *fuj* (*fie*), *ach* (*ah*), ...
55. *Numer* → *dva* (*two*), *tři* (*three*), *pět* (*five*), *třicet* (*thirty*), ...
56. *Pron* → *každý* (*every*), *některý* (*some*), ...
57. *Det* → *ten* (*that*), *tento* (*this*), ...

Modification Indices

Index	Type of modification	Example
0	*general relationship*	Father is *a tall man*. Father is *old*.
1	*author*	The letter is *from my father*.
2	*instrument*	He writes *with a pen*.
3	*interest*	The letter is *for my father*.
4	*extent*	He spent his money *to the last penny*.
5	*comparison*	He is *like me*. He is better *than you*.
6	*restriction*	Nobody was late *except me*.
7	*difference*	He is *two years* older.
8	*manner*	He sings *beautifully*.
9	*effect*	It went *to pieces*
10	*sociative*	He came *with his daughter*.
11	*possessive*	The book is *John's*.
12	*regard*	*As for his figure*, he is a tall man.
13	*origin*	He made it *out of wood*.
14	*cause*	She wept *for joy*.
15	*final*	Is there anything *to eat* here?
16	*real condition*	*With higher temperature* this liquid boils.
17	*unreal condition*	*If the temperature had not gone up*, it would not have thawed.
18	*concession*	It happened *in spite of his objections*.
19	*substitution*	He acts *for his father*.
20	*position*	He is *a chairman*.
21	*temp*$_1$ (*when?*)	He came *yesterday*.
22	*temp*$_2$ (*before when?*)	He came *before Christmas*.
23	*temp*$_3$ (*after when?*)	He came *after Christmas*.
24	*temp*$_4$ (*till when?*)	It lasted *until Christmas*.
25	*temp*$_5$ (*since when?*)	It has lasted *since Christmas*.
26	*temp*$_6$ (*how long?*)	It lasted *for two years*.
27	*temp*$_7$ (*how often?*)	This happens *every Sunday*.
28–68	*loc*$_{28}$ to *loc*$_{68}$ (cf. below)	
69	indirect question	I must find out *whether he came*.
70	vocative	Look here, *Jane!*

Modifications of place (*loc*$_i$):

Index	*Where*	*Which way*	*Whither*	*Whence*
28–31	*on, upon*	*over, across*	*on*	*from*
32–35	*on, at*	*on*	*on*	*from*
36–39	*in*	*through*	*into*	*from*
40–43	*at, by*	*by, along*	*to*	*from*
44–47	*over, above*	*over, above*	*over, above*	*from above*
48–51	*under*	*under*	*under*	*from underneath*
52–54	*in front of*		*in front of*	*from the front of*
55–57	*behind*		*behind*	*from behind*
58–60	*among*		*among*	*from among*
61–62	*between*		*between*	
63	*opposite*			
64	*past*			
65	*beside*			
66	*along*			
67	*round*			
68	*near*			

6.3 MODIFICATIONS OF THE TRANSDUCERS

6.3.1 THE MODIFIED FORM OF TRANSDUCER $\mathbf{T}_1$

The modification concerns certain syntagms the governor of which is the verb "to be" depending on a noun (see Section 6.1).

$\mathbf{T}_1=(V_1, V_2, V_0, S, P)$, where

$V_1=A_0 \cup F_0 \cup F'_0 \cup \{\#\}$

$V_2=F_0 \cup F'_0 \cup \tilde{F}_0 \cup_0 \tilde{F}' \cup \{+\} \cup \{a^{\mathbf{i}}_{\mathbf{x}}$, where $a \in A_1, \mathbf{i} \in \{\Lambda, r\}\}$,

$\mathbf{x} \in (\{\Lambda\} \cup A_1)$

$V_0=A_1 \cup A'_1 \cup \{\phi\} \cup \{\#\}$

$S=\{s_0, 1, 2\}$

P is given by the following table, modifying the table on page 81:

No.	I	WPS	IS	OS	RPS	O
1.	$\#$	Λ	s_0	1	$+$	$\#$
2.	f_1	Λ	1	1	f_1	Λ
3.	f'_2	Λ	1	1	f'_2	ϕ
4.	a_1	Λ	1	2	a_1	Λ
5.	Λ	$a^{\mathbf{i}_1}_{2,\mathbf{x}_1}$ f_3	2	1	$a^{\mathbf{i}_1}_{2,\mathbf{x}_1}$ $\tilde{f}_3$	ϕ
6.	Λ	$a^{\mathbf{i}_2}_{3,\mathbf{x}_2}$ f'_4	2	1	$a^{\mathbf{i}_2}_{3,\mathbf{x}_2}$ $\tilde{f}'_4$	a'_4

No.	I	WPS	IS	OS	RPS	O
7.	Λ	$a^{\mathbf{i}_3}_{5,\mathbf{x}_3}$ $a^{i_4}_{6,\mathbf{x}_4}$ $\tilde{f}_5$	2	2	$a^{\mathbf{i}_4}_{7,\mathbf{x}_5}$	$a^{i_5}_8$
8.	Λ	$a^{i_6}_{9,\mathbf{x}_6}$ $a^{\mathbf{i}_7}_{10,\mathbf{x}_7}$ $\tilde{f}'_6$	2	2	$a^{\mathbf{i}_8}_{11,\mathbf{x}_6}$	Λ
9.	Λ	$a^{\mathbf{i}_9}_{12,\mathbf{x}_8}$ $+$	2	3	Λ	$a^{\mathbf{i}_9}_{12}$
10.	#	Λ	3	s_0	Λ	#

In this table $a_1 \in A_0$, $a_2, ..., a_{12} \in A_1$, where $a_4 = \mathbf{q}_1 (f_4, a_3)$, $a_8 = \mathbf{q}_1 (f_5, a_5)$, $a_7 = \mathbf{t}_1 (a_5, f_5, a_6)$, $a_{11} = \mathbf{t}_1 (a_{10}, f_6, a_9)$, $\mathbf{i}_1, \mathbf{i}_2, \mathbf{i}_3, \mathbf{i}_4, \mathbf{i}_6, \mathbf{i}_7, \mathbf{i}_9 \in \{\Lambda, r\}$, $\mathbf{x}_1, \mathbf{x}_2, \mathbf{x}_3, \mathbf{x}_4, \mathbf{x}_6, \mathbf{x}_7, \mathbf{x}_8 \in A_1 \cup \{\Lambda\}$ and the following statements hold:
if $\mathbf{x}_3$ is related to a_6 and if $\mathbf{i}_3 = r$, then $\mathbf{i}_5 = r$; in other cases $\mathbf{i}_5 = \Lambda$;
if $a_9 \in Be$, $\mathbf{i}_6 = \Lambda$, $a_{10} \subset Adject \cup Num$, then $\mathbf{i}_8 \in \{r, \Lambda\}$; in other cases $\mathbf{i}_8 = \Lambda$;
if $a_6 \in Be$, $\mathbf{x}_4 = \Lambda$, $a_5 \in N$, then $\mathbf{x}_5 = a_5$; in other cases $\mathbf{x}_5 = \Lambda$.

We say that two terms *a*, *b* are related, iff the first index of *a* is a zero and *a* has no third index, while its other parts are identical with those of *b* (e.g. the symbols $jednotka_{0,\,pl}$ and $jednotka_{5,\,pl}$).

The symbols *N*, *Adject*, *Num* and others symbolize subsets of the set A_1; *Num* symbolizes the set *pět, šest, sedm, ..., třicet, ...* (the set of numerals *five, six, seven, ..., thirty, ...*). Such symbols as *N*, *Adject*, *Num* henceforth denote elements of partitions of the sets A_1, A_2, A_3, A_4, that is, sets of word-forms at individual stages of the description (see Section 2.1.3 for some of these sets).

As we shall see, this modified version of the automaton $\mathbf{T}_1$ is non-deterministic: in some steps of some computations it is possible to insert either a term without a superscript or the same term with the superscript *r* (see above about the index $\mathbf{i}_8$). If a term with a superscript *r* is inserted, then the transducer $\mathbf{T}_2$ (if also some other conditions are fulfilled concerning beside others further modification of the syntagm in question) translates this syntagm to the phenogrammatical level as a congruent adjectival attributive (e.g. *větší dávka —a larger dose*—in the sentence of Section 6.5); otherwise it is translated as a relative clause (but see Section 3.4).

6.3.2 ADDENDA TO TRANSDUCER $\mathbf{T}_2$

Let us denote the set $A_2 \cup \{!a!, ?a?, \S a\S\ \&a\&;$ where $a \in A_2\}$ by B_2; then it will be sufficient to add Rules 22–31 to Rules 1–21; to extend the range of $a_5, ..., a_{19}, a_{21}, ..., a_{28}$ to B_2; to restrict the range of a_1 to $A_0 — Be^r$; in these new rules $a_{30} \in Be^r$, $a_{35} \in A_1 — Num$, $a_{37} \in Num$, $a_{41} \in Num$, $a_{43} \in A_2 — Num$, $a_{31}, a_{32}, a_{33}, a_{34}, a_{36}, a_{38}, a_{39}, a_{40}, a_{42}, a_{44} \in A_2$; $b_1 \in \mathbf{t}_2 (a_{36}, a_{35})$. Let $p_{a,\,\mathbf{x},\,b}$, $q_{\mathbf{y}}$ be the forms of symbols a_{38}, a_{37}, respectively; then $\mathbf{t}\,(a_{38}, a_{37}) = q_{a,\,b}$, $\mathbf{t}\,(a_{38}) = p_{0,\,b,\,attr}$.

Addenda to the defining relation of $\mathbf{T}_2$:

No.	I	RPS	IS	OS	WPS	O
22.	a_{30}	a_{31}	1	1	$?a_{31}?$	Λ
23.	a_{32}	$?a_{33}?$	1	1	$!a_{33}!$	Λ
24.	ϕ	$!a_{34}!$	1	1	$\S a_{34}\S$	Λ
25.	a'_{35}	$\S a_{36}\S$	1	1	b_1 $\S a_{36}\S$	Λ
26.	a'_{37}	$\S a_{38}\S$	1	1	$\&\mathbf{t}(a_{38}, a_{37})\&$ $\S\mathbf{t}(a_{38})\S$	Λ
27.	ϕ	$\&a_{39}\&$ $\S a_{40}\S$	1	1	$\ominus_{a_{39}}$ $\S a_{40}\S$	a_{39}
28.	ϕ	$\ominus_{a_{41}}$ $\S a_{42}\S$	1	1	a_{42} $\otimes$	Λ
29.	ϕ	$\ominus_{a_{43}}$ $\S a_{44}\S$	1	1	a_{44} O	Λ
30.	Λ	$\otimes$	3	3	Λ	ϕ'
31.	Λ	$\otimes$	4	4	Λ	ϕ'

6.3.3 THE MODIFIED FORM OF TRANSDUCER $\mathbf{T}_4$

$\mathbf{T}_4=\langle V_1, V_2, V_0, S, P\rangle$, where
$V_1=A_3 \cup A_3' \cup \{\phi\}$,
$V_2=B \cup B^{\circ} \cup B^{\emptyset} \cup \{\otimes\}$, where
$B^{\circ}=\{\ominus_b \mid b \in B\}$, $B^{\emptyset}=\{\emptyset_b \mid b \in B\}$,
$B=A_4 \cup A_4^*$, $A_4^*=\{a^* \mid a \in A_4\}$
$V_0=A_4 \cup \pi$, where π is a set of prepositions,
$S=\{s_0, 1, 2, \tilde{2}, \bar{2}, 3, 4\}$;

We take * to be an idempotent operator, that is, $(a^*)^*=a^*$ for each $a \in A_4$. The symbol p used in the table of the defining relation is a prescription that assigns the preposition p_a to each $a \in A_p$ ($A_p \subset A_4$) and an empty string to each $a \in A^*_4 \cup (A_4-A_p)$. The symbols $a_1, a_3, a_{14}, a_{16}, a_{27}$, denotes arbitrary elements from A_3; the symbols $a_2, a_6, a_{13}, a_{15}, a_{17}, \ldots, a_{26}, a_{30}, a_{31}, a_{33}, \ldots, a_{43}, a_{45}, a_{46}, a_{48}, a_{49}$ denote arbitrary elements from B; furthermore $a_4 \in A_3$, $a_5 \in B$ and either $a_4 \notin A_{ne\check{z}}$ or $a_5 \notin Adject_{comp}$; $a_{28} \in A_{ne\check{z}}$, $a_{29} \in Adject_{comp}$, $a_{32} \in N$; $a_{44}, a_{47} \in B-N$; $A_{ne\check{z}}$ is the set of those symbols from A_3 of which the first index is the number 5 (e.g. *třicet*$_{5,\,adv}$), $b_1 \in \mathbf{t}_4(a_2, a_1)$, $b_2 \in \mathbf{t}_4(a_7, a_6)$, $b_3 \in \mathbf{t}_4(a_9, a_8)$, $b_4 \in \mathbf{t}_4(a_{12}, a_{11})$, $b_5 \in \mathbf{t}_4(a_{15}, a_{14})$, $b_6 \in \mathbf{t}_4(a_{17}, a_{16})$, $b_7 \in \mathbf{t}_4(a_{29}, a_{28})$, $b_8 \in \mathbf{t}_4(a_{34}, a_{33})$, $b_9 \in \mathbf{t}_4(a_{37}, a_{36})$, $b_{10} \in \mathbf{t}_4(a_{40}, a_{39})$.

The defining relation:

No.	I	RPS	IS	OS	WPS	O
1.	#	Λ	s_0	1	+	#
2.	a_1	a_2	1	1	b_1 a_2^*	p_{a_2}

No.	I	RPS	IS	OS	WPS	O
3.	a_3	$+$	1	1	a_3^*	pa_3
4.	a'_4	a_5	1	2	a_4 a_5^*	$pa_5\ a_5$
5.	Λ	a_6 a_7 $+$	2	1	b_2 $\emptyset a_7$ $+$	Λ
6.	Λ	a_8 a_9 a_{10}	2	1	b_3 $\emptyset a_9$ a_{10}	Λ
7.	Λ	a_{11} a_{12} $\emptyset a_{13}$	2	1	b_4 $\emptyset a_{12}$ $\emptyset a_{13}$	Λ
8.	a'_{14}	$\ominus a_{15}$	1	1	b_5 $\emptyset a_{15}$	Λ
9.	a_{16}	$\ominus a_{17}$	1	1	b_6 $\emptyset a_{17}$	Λ
10.	ϕ	a_{18}	1	3	Λ	$pa_{18}\ a_{18}$
11.	Λ	a_{19}	3	1	a_{19}	Λ
12.	Λ	$\emptyset a_{20}$	3	1	$\ominus a_{20}$	Λ
13.	ϕ	$\ominus a_{21}$ a_{22}	1	1	a_{22}	Λ
14.	ϕ	$\ominus a_{23}$ $\emptyset a_{24}$	1	1	$\ominus a_{24}$	Λ
15.	$\#$	a_{25}	1	4	Λ	$pa_{25}\ a_{25}$
16.	Λ	$+$	4	s_0	Λ	$\#$
17.	$\#$	$\ominus a_{26}$ $+$	1	s_0	Λ	$\#$
18.	a'_{27}	$+$	1	1	a_{27} $+$	Λ
19.	a'_{28}	a_{29}	1	$\tilde{2}$	b_7 a_{29}	Λ
20.	Λ	a_{30} a_{31} a_{32}	$\tilde{2}$	$\bar{2}$	a_{30} a_{32}^*	$pa_{32}\ a_{31}$
21.	Λ	a_{33} a_{34} a_{35}	$\bar{2}$	1	b_8 $\emptyset a_{34}$ $\otimes$ a_{35}	a_{34}
22.	Λ	a_{36} a_{37} $\emptyset a_{38}$	$\bar{2}$	1	b_9 $\emptyset a_{37}$ $\otimes$ $\emptyset a_{38}$	Λ

No.	I	RPS	IS	OS	WPS	O
23.	Λ	a_{39} a_{40} $+$	$\bar{2}$	1	b_{10} $\emptyset a_{40}$ $\otimes$ $+$	Λ
24.	ϕ	$\ominus a_{41}$ $\otimes$	1	1	$\ominus a_{41}$	Λ
25.	Λ	a_{42} a_{43} a_{44}	$\tilde{2}$	2	a_{42} $\overset{*}{a}_{43}$ a_{44}	$p_{a_{43}}\, a_{43}$
26.	Λ	a_{45} a_{46} $\emptyset a_{47}$	$\tilde{2}$	2	a_{45} $\overset{*}{a}_{46}$ $\emptyset a_{47}$	$p_{a_{46}}\, a_{46}$
27.	Λ	a_{48} a_{49} $+$	$\tilde{2}$	2	a_{48} $\overset{*}{a}_{49}$ $+$	$p_{a_{49}}\, a_{49}$

6.4 MAPPINGS

In this section we present tables illustrating the mappings concerning modifications of symbols performed by the transducers. The connection of these mappings with the transducers is given by their defining relation (see Sections 5.2 and 6.3); for the linguistic interpretation see Section 2.2.4.

The tables include only some examples. They have the forms of schemata: $b_{\mathbf{x}}$ is an arbitrary symbol from A_1; **x** is the string of its indices. If, for instance, $b_{\mathbf{x}} \in A_1$ is a verb, then—according to Table 1b—$\mathbf{e}\,(R_g, b_{\mathbf{x}}) = b_{\mathbf{x},pat}$ if *pat* is not contained in **x**; each of the indices *ag*, *pat*, *exp* is added at most once to the same occurence of a word-form.

In Table 2[2] we write *V*, *pat* etc. instead of V_{pat} and the like; only the relevant indices are given here. In the leftmost column the indices of the modified word-form (from A_1) are given; **x** is written as an abbreviation for index 1 together with a modal index other than *vol* (see Section 3.2). The heading of the table contains the relevant subsets of governing word-forms (from A_2), according to which the modifications are made. The rows and columns of the table (as well as those of Table 3) are ordered in such a way that cases with fewer relevant indices are preceded by cases with more; in other words, when searching for a modification, one has to go down through the leftmost column and to the right through the heading to find the first convenient subset. According to this table the lexical semantemes are changed into the corresponding tagmemes; for instance a verbal semanteme is changed either into a verbal tagmeme, or into the tagmeme of a noun (N_V) having the same lexical meaning as the verb. Similarly, Ad_A denotes an adverb corresponding to an adjective (e.g. *quickly* to *quick*, *well* to *good*). The index adv_{act} denotes the actor of a passive verb (as a sentence part). The indices *subj*, *obj*, *attr*, *adv*, *pred* (i.e., predicate nominal) symbolize other sentence parts. The index *exp* is supposed to be deleted, which is not specified in the table. Numerals of the type *pět* (*five*) are included here in the subset of nouns (*N*). The index *gen* denotes the general subject (it is attached as a suffix to a verb having this subject; see Section 3.2); the symbol—stands at the head of the column containing modified independent word-forms (i.e. predicates of main clauses, or finite verbal forms included in such predicates). Many questions concerning this table still remain open; for example, the table in this form does not account for impersonal passive constructions, and in general for verbs that can be expanded by a goal but have no personal passive forms (as *škodí* in our example; see Section 6.5).

TABLE 1a

Mapping $\mathbf{q}_1: F_0 \times A_1 \to A_1$

	R_a	R_g	R_m	R_n	R_v
b_x	$b_{x,a}$	$b_{x,g}$	$b_{x,m}$	$b_{x,n}$	$b_{x,v}$

TABLE 1b

Mapping $\mathbf{e}: F_0 \times A_1 \to A_1$

	R_a	R_g	R_m	R_n	R_v
V	*ag*	*pat*	*exp*	*exp*	—
N	—	—	*exp*	—	—
Adject	—	—	—	—	—
Numer	—	—	*exp*	—	—
Adverb	—	—	*exp*	—	—

6.5 EXAMPLE

First we give the derivation of a proposition, in a well-known form (the number on the left is that of the rule applied in the given step; the boundary symbols are omitted). It is a proposition corresponding to the Czech sentence *Větší dávka než třicet jednotek člověku škodí.* (lit. transl. *A larger dose than thirty units injures a man.*)

Proposition

1 *Declar*

2 $Pred_{0,0,imperf,ind,gnom,declar}$

5 $Pred_{0,0,imperf,ind,gnom,declar,1}$

6 $NP_{0,0}\ VP^{0}_{0,0,imperf,ind,gnom,declar,1}\ R_a$

12 $NP_{0,0}\ NP_{0,0}\ VP^{2}_{0,0,\,imperf,\,ind,\,gnom,\,declar,\,1}\ R_g\ R_a$

13 $NP_{0,0}\ NP_{0,0}\ V^{semitrans}_{0,0,\,imperf,\,ind,\,gnom,\,declar,\,1}\ R_g\ R_a$

17, 17 $Nom_{0,0},\ Nom_{0,0},\ V^{semitrans}_{0,0,\,imperf,\,ind,\,gnom,\,declar,\,1}\ R_g\ R_a$

18, 18 $N_{0,0}\ N_{0,0}\ V^{semitrans}_{0,0,\,inper,\,ind,\,gnom,\,declar,1}\ R_g\ R_a$

19 $Pred_{0,\,simult,\,imperf,\,ind,\,gnom,\,0}\ N_{0,0}\ R_m\ N_{0,0}$
$V^{semitrans}_{0,0,\,imperf,\,ind,\,gnom\ declar,\,1}\ R_g\ R_a$

25 $Pred_{0,\,simult,\,imperf,\,ind,\,gnom,\,0}\ NP_{5,\,pl}\ R'_m\ N_{0,0}\ R_m \ldots$

5 $Pred_{0,\,simult,\,imperf,\,ind,\,gnom,\,0,\,1}\ NP_{5,\,pl}\ R'_m\ N_{0,0}\ R_m \ldots$

6 $NP_{0,0}\ NP_{0,\,simult,\,imperf,\,ind,\,gnom,\,0,\,1}\ R_a\ NP_{5,\,pl}\ R'_m\ N_{0,0}\ R_m \ldots$

8, 17, 17 $Nom_{0,0}\ Be_{0,\,simult,\,imperf,\,ind,\,gnom,\,0,\,1}\ Adj\ R'_n\ R_a\ Nom_{5,\,pl}\ R'_m\ N_{0,0}$
$R_m \ldots$

18, 18 $N_{0,0}\ Be_{0,\,simult,\,imperf,\,ind,\,gnom,\,0,\,1}\ Adj\ R'_n\ R_a\ N_{5,\,pl}\ R'_m\ N_{0,0}\ R_m \ldots$

19 $N_{0,0}\ Be_{0,\,simult,\,imperf,\,ind,\,gnom,\,0,\,1}\ Adj\ R'_n\ R_a$
$Pred_{0,\,simult,\,imperf,\,ind,\,gnom,\,0}\ N_{5,\,pl}\ R_m\ R'_m\ N_{0,0}\ R_m \ldots$

5 $N_{0,0}\ Be_{0,\,simult,\,imperf,\,ind,\,gnom,\,0,\,1}\ Adj\ R'_n\ R_a$
$Pred_{0,\,simult,\,imperf,\,ind,\,gnom,\,0,\,1}\ N_{5,\,pl}\ R_m\ R'_m\ N_{0,0}\ R_m \ldots$

6 $N_{0,0}\ Be_{0,\,simult,\,imperf,\,ind,\,gnom,\,0,\,1}\ Adj\ R'_n\ R_a\ NP_{0,\,pl}$
$PQ_{0,\,simult,\,imperf,\,ind,\,gnom,\,0,\,1}\ R_a\ N_{5,\,pl}\ R_m\ R'_m\ N_{0,0}\ R_m \ldots$

9, 17 $N_{0,0}\ Be_{0,\,simult,\,imperf,\,ind,\,gnom,\,0,\,1}\ Adj\ R'_n\ R_a\ Nom_{0,\,pl}$
$Be_{0,\,simult,\,imperf,\,ind,\,gnom,\,0,\,1}\ Numer\ R'_n\ R_a\ N_{5,\,pl}\ R_m\ R'_m\ N_{0,0}\ R_m \ldots$

18, 20 $N_{0,0}\ Be_{0,\,simult,\,imperf,\,ind,\,gnom,\,0,\,1}\ Adject_{comp}\ R'_n\ R_a\ N_{0,\,pl}$
$Be_{0,\,simult,\,imperf,\,ind,\,gnom,\,0,\,1}\ Numer\ R'_n\ R_a\ N_{5,\,pl}\ R_m\ R'_m$
$N_{0,0}\ R_m\ N_{0,0}\ V^{semitrans}_{0,0,\,imperf,\,ind,\,gnom,\,declar,\,1}\ R_g\ R_a$

selectional rules *dávka*$_{0,0}$ *je*$_{0,\,simult,\,imperf,\,ind,\,gnom,\,0,\,1}$ *velký*$_{comp}$ $R'_n\ R_a$ *jednotka*$_{0,\,pl}$
je$_{0,\,simult,\,imperf,\,ind,\,gnom,\,0,\,1}$ *třicet* $R'_n\ R_a$ *jednotka*$_{5,\,pl}$
$R_m\ R'_m$ *dávka*$_{0,0}$ R_m *člověk*$_{0,0}$ *škodí*$_{0,0,\,imperf,\,ind,\,gnom,\,declar,\,1}$ $R_g\ R_a$

The string derived in this way is a representation of the sentence on the tectogrammatical level. It is then translated to a representation on the phenogrammatical level by transducers $\mathbf{T}_1$ and $\mathbf{T}_2$. The pass through transducer $\mathbf{T}_1$ is given in full on pages 108 and 109.

After this pass we obtain the string
$\#\ \phi$ *člověk*$_{0,\,0,\,g}$ $\phi\ \phi\ \phi\ \phi\ \phi$ *třicet*$'_n$ ϕ *jednotka*$_{0,\,pl,\,a}$ *je*$^{r}_{0,\,simult,\,imperf,\,gnom,\,ind,\,0,\,1\,ag,\,m}$ *jednotka*$'_{5,\,pl,\,exp,\,m}$ ϕ *velký*$'_{comp,\,n}$ ϕ *dávka*$_{0,\,0,\,a}$ *je*$^{r}_{0,\,simult,\,imperf,\,gnom,\,ind,\,0,\,1,\,ag,\,m}$ *dávka*$_{0,\,0,\,exp,\,a}$ *škodí*$_{0,\,0,\,imperf,\,pres,\,ind,\,declar,\,1,\,pat,\,ag}$ $\#$.
By the pass through transducer $\mathbf{T}_2$ this string is changed into $\#$ *velký*$_{comp,\,attr}$ *třicet*$_{5,\,adv}$ *jednotka*$_{0,\,pl,\,attr}$ $\phi'\ \phi'$ *dávka*$_{0,\,0,\,subj}$ ϕ *člověk*$_{0,\,0,\,obj}$ *škodí*$_{0,\,imperf,\,pres,\,ind,\,declar,\,1}$ $\phi\ \phi\ \#$.
This string is a representation of the sentence on the phenogrammatical level and is translated to a representation on the morphemic level by transducers $\mathbf{T}_3$ and $\mathbf{T}_4$.
By a pass through $\mathbf{T}_3$ the following string is obtained:
$\#\ \phi$ *člověk*$_{0,\,0,\,obj}$ $\phi\ \phi\ \phi\ \phi$ *jednotka*$_{0',\,pl,\,attr}$ *třicet*$'_{5,\,adv}$ *velký*$_{comp,\,attr}$ *dávka*$_{0,0,\,subj}$ *škodí*$_{0,\,0,\,imperf,\,pres,\,ind,\,declar,\,1}$ $\#$.

By a pass through T_4 we obtain:
velký $_{comp,\ f,\ nom}$ *dávka* $_{nom}$ *než třicet* $_{nom}$ *jednotka* $_{pl,\ genit}$ *člověk* $_{0,\ dat}$ *škodí* $_{0,\ 0,\ imperf,\ pres,\ ind,\ declar,\ 1}$ #, which is the representation of the sentence on the morphemic level.

NOTE

1. The English words here and in the following lists do not give a full picture of the Czech examples; they can serve the reader only by improving his orientation.
2. Tables 2 and 3 are given on pp. 110-112.

(For the sake of brevity, all the indices that do not change, originate or disappear during the pass through the transducers are omitted.)

n	**a**$_n$	**b**$_n$	s_n	s^*_n	**b**$^*_n$	**a**$^*_n$	Number of the rule applied	Internal string after the application of the rule
1	$\#$	Λ	s_0	1	$+$	$\#$	1	$+$
2	R_a	Λ	1	1	R_a	Λ	2	$+R_a$
3	R_g	Λ	1	1	R_g	Λ	2	$+R_a\ R_g$
4	*škodí*	Λ	1	2	*škodí*	Λ	4	$+R_a\ R_g$ *škodí*
5	Λ	R_g *škodí*	2	1	$\tilde{R}_g$ *škodí*	ϕ	5	$+R_a\ \tilde{R}_g$ *škodí*
6	*člověk*	Λ	1	2	*člověk*	Λ	4	$+R_a\ \tilde{R}_g$ *škodí člověk*
7	Λ	$\tilde{R}_g$ *škodí člověk*	2	2	*škodí*$_{pat}$	*člověk*$_g$	7	$+R_a$ *škodí* $_{pat}$
8	Λ	R_a *škodí*$_{pat}$	2	1	$\tilde{R}_a$ *škodí*$_{pat}$	ϕ	5	$+\tilde{R}_a$ *škodí*$_{pat}$
9	R_m	Λ	1	1	R_m	Λ	2	$+\tilde{R}_a$ *škodí*$_{pat}$ R_m
10	*dávka*	Λ	1	2	*dávka*	Λ	4	$+\tilde{R}_a$ *škodí*$_{pat}$ R_m *dávka*
11	Λ	R_m *dávka*	2	1	$\tilde{R}_m$ *dávka*	ϕ	5	...*dávka*
12	R'_m	Λ	1	1	R'_m	ϕ	3	...*dávka* R'_m
13	R_m	Λ	1	1	R_m	Λ	2	...*dávka* $R'_m\ R_m$
14	*jednotka*	Λ	1	2	*jednotka*	Λ	4	...*dávka* $R_m\ R_m$ *jednotka*
15	Λ	R_m *jednotka*	2	1	$\tilde{R}_m$ *jednotka*	ϕ	5	...*dávka* $R'_m\ \tilde{R}_m$ *jednotka*
16	R_a	Λ	1	1	R_a	Λ	2	...*dávka* $R'_m\ \tilde{R}_m$ *jednotka* R_a
17	R'_n	Λ	1	1	R'_n	ϕ	3	...*dávka* $R'_m\ \tilde{R}_m$ *jednotka* $R_a\ R'_n$
18	*třicet*	Λ	1	2	*třicet*	Λ	4	...*jednotka* $R_a\ R'_n$ *třicet*
19	Λ	R'_n *třicet*	2	1	$\tilde{R}'_n$ *třicet*	*třicet*$'_n$	6	...*jednotka* $R_a\ \tilde{R}'_n$ *třicet*

20	*je*	Λ	1	2	*je*	Λ	4	...*jednotka* R_a $\tilde{R}'_n$ *třicet je*
21	Λ	$\tilde{R}'_n$ *třicet je*	2	2	je^r	Λ	8	...*jednotka* R_a je^r
22	Λ	R_a je^r	2	1	$\tilde{R}_a$ je^r	ϕ	5	...*jednotka* $\tilde{R}_a$ je^r
23	*jednotka*	Λ	1	2	*jednotka*	Λ	4	...*jednotka* $\tilde{R}_a$ je^r *jednotka*
24	Λ	$\tilde{R}_a$ je^r *jednotka*	2	2	$je^r_{ag,\ jednotka}$	$jednotka_a$	7	...*jednotka* $je^r_{ag,\ jednotka}$
25	Λ	$\tilde{R}_m$ *jednotka* $je^r_{ag,\ jednotka}$	2	2	$jednotka_{exp}$	$je^r_{ag,\ m}$	7	...$jednotka_{exp}$
26	Λ	R'_m $jednotka_{exp}$	2	1	$\tilde{R}'_m$ $jednotka_{exp}$	$jednotka'_{exp,\ m}$	6	...$jednotka_{\ exp}$
27	R_a	Λ	1	1	R_a	Λ	2	...$jednotka_{\ exp}$ R_a
28	R'_n	Λ	1	1	R'_n	ϕ	3	...$jednotka_{exp}$ R_a R'_n
29	*velký*	Λ	1	2	*velký*	Λ	4	...$jednotka_{exp}$ R_a R'_n *velký*
30	Λ	R'_n *velký*	2	1	$\tilde{R}'_n$ *velký*	$velký'_n$	6	...*jednotka* R_a $\tilde{R}'_n$ *velký*
31	*je*	Λ	1	2	*je*	Λ	4	...*jednotka* R_a $\tilde{R}'_n$ *velký je*
32	Λ	$\tilde{R}'_n$ *velký je*	2	2	je^r	Λ	8	...*jednotka* R_a je^r
33	Λ	R_a je^r	2	1	$\tilde{R}_a$ je^r	ϕ	5	...*jednotka* $\tilde{R}_a$ je^r
34	*dávka*	Λ	1	2	*dávka*	Λ	4	...*jednotka* $\tilde{R}_a$ je^r *dávka*
35	Λ	$\tilde{R}_a$ je^r *dávka*	2	2	$je^r_{ag,\ davka}$	$dávka_a$	7	+ $\tilde{R}_a$ *škodí* $\tilde{R}'_n$ *dávka* R'_n *jednotka* $je^r_{ag,\ davka}$
36	Λ	$\tilde{R}'_n$ *jednotka* $je^r_{ag,\ davka}$	2	2	$je^r_{ag,\ davka}$	Λ	7	+ $\tilde{R}_a$ $škodí_{\ pat}$ $\tilde{R}_m$ *dávka* $je^r_{ag,\ davka}$
37	Λ	$\tilde{R}_m$ *dávka* $je^r_{ag,\ davka}$	2	2	$dávka_{exp}$	$je^r_{ag\ m}$	7	+ $\tilde{R}_a$ $škodí_{pat}$ $dávka_{exp}$
38	Λ	$\tilde{R}_a$ $škodí_{pat}dávka_{exp}$	2	2	$škodí_{pat,\ ag}$	$dávka_{,\ exp,\ a}$	7	+ $škodí_{pat,\ ag}$
39	Λ	+ $škodí_{pat,\ ag}$	2	3	Λ	$škodí_{pat,\ ag}$	9	Λ
40	#	Λ	3	s_0	Λ	#	10	

TABLE 2

Mapping t_2: $A_2 \times A_1 \rightarrow A_2$

	$V, 1, pass$	$V, 2$	$V, 1$	N_V	N	$Adject$	—	...
V, **x** pat, ag, a	V, adv_{act} $V, pass, adv_{act}$ N_V, adv_{act}		$V, subj$ $V, pass, subj$ $N_V, subj$	$V, attr$ $V, pass, attr$ $N_V, attr$				...
V, **x**, pat, ag, g	$V, subj$ $V, pass, subj$ $N_V, subj$	V, obj $V, pass, obj$ N_V, obj	V, obj $V, pass, obj$ N_V, obj	$V, attr$ $V, pass, attr$ $N_V, attr$				...
V, **x**, pat, ag, m	V, adv $V, pass, adv$ N_V, adv	V, adv $V, pass, adv$ N_V, adv	V, adv $V, pass, adv$ N_V, adv	$V, attr$ $V, pass, attr$ $N_V attr$	$V, attr$ $V, pass, attr$ $Adject_V, attr$	V, adv $V, pass, adv$ N_V, adv		...
V, **x**, pat, ag							V $V, pass$	
V, **x**, pat, a	V, gen, adv_{act} $V, pass, adv_{act}$ N_V, adv_{act}		$V, gen, subj$ $V, pass, subj$ $N_V, subj$	$V, gen, attr$ $V, pass, attr$ $N_V, attr$				...
V, **x**, pat, g	$V, gen, subj$ $V, pass, subj$ $N_V, subj$	V, gen, obj $V, pass, obj$ N_V, obj	V, gen, obj $V, pass, obj$ N_V, obj	$V, gen, attr$ $V, pass, attr$ $N_V, attr$				...
V, **x**, pat, m	V, gen, adv $V, pass, adv$ N_V, adv	V, gen, adv $V, pass, adv$ N_V, adv	V, gen, adv $V, pass, adv$ N_V, adv	$V, gen, attr$ $V, pass, attr$ $N_V, attr$	$V, gen, attr$ $V, pass, attr$ $Adject_V, attr$	V, gen, adv $V, pass, adv$ N_V, adv		...
V, **x**, pat							V, gen $V, pass$	

V, ag, a	V, *adv*$_{act}$ N_V, *adv*$_{act}$		V, *subj* N_V, *subj*	V, *attr* N_V, *attr*			...
V, ag, g	V, *subj* N_V, *subj*	V, *obj* N_V, *obj*	V, *obj* N_V, *obj*	V, *attr* N_V, *attr*			...
V, ag, m	V, *adv* N_V, *adv*	V, *adv* N_V, *adv*	V, *adv* N_V, *adv*	V, *attr* N_V, *attr*	V, *attr* *Adject*$_V$, *attr*	V, *adv* N_V, *adv*	...
V, ag							*V*
V, a	V, *gen*, *adv*$_{act}$ N_V, *adv*$_{act}$		V, *gen*, *subj* N_V, *subj*	V, *gen*, *attr* N_V, *attr*			...
V, g	V, *gen*, *subj* N_V, *subj*	V, *gen*, *obj* N_V, *obj*	V, *gen*, *obj* N_V, *obj*	V, *gen*, *attr* N_V, *attr*			...
V, m	V, *gen*, *adv* N_V, *adv*	V, *gen*, *adv* N_V, *adv*	V, *gen*, *adv* N_V, *adv*	V, *gen*, *attr* N_V, *attr*	V, *gen*, *attr* *Adject*$_V$, *attr*	V, *gen*, *adv* N_V, *adv*	...
V							*V*
N, a	*N*, *adv*$_{act}$	*N, voc*	*N, subj*	*N, attr*			...
N, g	*N, subj*	*N, obj*	*N, obj*	*N, attr*			...
N, m	*N, adv*	*N, adv*	*N, adv*	*N, attr*	*N, attr*	*N, adv*	...
N, n		*N, pred*	*N, pred*		*N, attr*		...
N, v	*N, voc*	*N, voc*	*N, voc*				...
N							*N*
Adject, m	*Ad*$_A$, *adv*	*Ad*$_A$, *adv*	*Ad*$_A$, *adv*	*Adject, attr*	*Adject, attr*		...
Adject, n		*Adject, pred*	*Adject, pred*	*Adject, attr*	*Adject, attr*		
.							
.							
.							

TABLE 3

Mapping t_4: $A_4 \times A_3 \rightarrow A_4$

	V_4	V_3	N_f, *pl*, *nom*	N_f, *nom*	*Num*, *nom*	...*Adject*, *comp*, *nom*	...—
N, 5, *adv*			*N*, *nom*, *jako*	*N*, *nom*, *jako*		*N*, *nom*, *než*	
N, *obj*	*N*, *acc*	*N*, *dat*					
N, *subj*	*N*, *nom*	*N*, *nom*					
N, *attr*			*N*, *genit*	*N*, *genit*	*N*, *genit*		
.							
.							
.							
N							*N*, *nom*
Num, 5, *adv*			*Num*, *nom*, *jako*	*Num*, *nom*, *jako*	*Num*, *nom*, *jako*	*Num*, *nom*, *než*	
Num, *obj*	*Num*, *acc*	*Num*, *dat*					
.							
.							
.							
Adject, *attr*			*Adject*, *f*, *pl*, *nom*	*Adject*, *f*, *nom*			
.							
.							
.							
V, *gnom*, *obj*	*V*, *pres*, *že*						
V, *gnom*							*V*, *pres*
.							
.							
.							

Note: Here *f* denotes the feminine gender, V_4 symbolizes the subset of verbs governing the accusative, etc.

BIBLIOGRAPHY

Apresjan, Ju. D. (1967), "Eksperimental'noje issledovanije semantiki russkogo glagola," Moskva.

Bar-Hillel, Y. (1950), "On Syntactical Categories," *Journ. of Symbolic Logic* 15, 1–16, reprinted in Bar-Hillel (1964).

——— (1964), "Language and Information," Reading (Mass.)—Jerusalem.

——— (1967), "Dictionaries and Meaning Rules," *Foundations of Language* 3, 409–414.

Benešová, E. (in press), "Nekotoryje voprosy po opisaniju modal'nosti," *Prague Studies in Mathematical Linguistics* 3.

Bierwisch, M. (1962), "Über den theoretischen Status des Morphems," *Studia grammatica*, Vol. 1, pp. 51–89.

Bloch, B. (1941), "Phonemic Overlapping," *American Speech*, Vol. 16, pp. 278–284, quoted from M. Joos (ed.), *Readings in Linguistics*, New York 1958, 2nd ed., pp. 93–96.

Chomsky, N. (1955), "The Logical Structure of Linguistic Theory," mimeographed.

——— (1957), "Syntactic Structures," The Hague.

——— (1959), "On Certain Formal Properties of Grammars," *Information and Control*, Vol. 2, pp. 137–167.

——— (1961), "On the Notion 'Rule of Grammar' ", *Structure of Language and Its Mathematical Aspects* (R. Jakobson, ed.), Proc. of the Symp. in Appl. Math., Vol. 12, pp. 6–24.

——— (1962a), "Logical Basis of Linguistic Theory," *Proc. of the Ninth Intern. Congress of Linguists* (G. Lunt, ed.), The Hague 1964, pp. 914–978.

——— (1962b), "Explanatory Models in Linguistics," *Logic, Methodology and Philosophy of Science* (E. Nagel, P. Suppes, A. Tarski, eds.), Proc. of the 1960 Intern. Congress, Stanford, pp. 528–550.

——— (1963), "Formal Properties of Grammars," *Handbook of Mathematical Psychology* Vol. 2 (R. Bush, E. Galanter, D. Luce, eds.), New York, pp. 323–418.

——— (1965), "Aspects of the Theory of Syntax," Cambridge (Mass.).

Čulík, K. (1965a), "Ispol'zovanije abstraktnoj semantiki i teorii grafov v mnogoznachnykh perevodnykh slovarjakh," *Problemy kibernetiki*, Vol. 13, pp. 221–232.

——— (1965b), "Některé problémy teorie jazyků" (Some Problems of the Theory of Languages), *Kybernetika a její využití* (Cybernetics and Its Applications), Prague, pp. 276–290.

Curry, H. B. (1961), "Some Logical Aspects of Grammatical Structure," *Structure of Language and Its Mathematical Aspects* (R. Jakobson, ed.), Proc. of the Symp. in Appl. Math., Vol. 12, pp. 56–68.

Daneš, F. (1957), "Intonace a věta ve spisovné češtině" (The Sentence Intonation in Standard Czech), Prague.

——— (1960), "Sentence Intonation from a Functional Point of View," *Word*, Vol. 16, pp. 34–54.

——— (1963), "Větný model a větný vzorec" (Syntactic Model and Syntactic Pattern), *Československé přednášky pro V. mezinárodní sjezd slavistů* (*Czechoslovak Contributions to The Fifth Intern. Congress of Slavists*), Prague, pp. 115–124.

——— (1964a), "A Three-Level Approach to Syntax," *Travaux linguistiques de Prague*, Vol. 1, pp. 225–240.

——— (1964b), "Opyt teoreticheskoj interpretacii sintaksicheskoj omonimii," *Voprosy jazykoznanija*, Vol. 13, no. 6, pp. 3–16.

Dokulil, M. (1962), "Teorie odvozování slov" (Theory of Word Derivation), *Tvoření slov v češtině* (*Word Formation in Czech*), Vol. 1, Prague.

———, and F. Daneš (1958), "K tzv. významové a mluvnické stavbě věty" (On the So-called Semantic and Grammatical Structures of the Sentence), *O vědeckém poznání soudobých jazyků* (*On the Research into Contemporary Languages*), Prague, pp. 231–246.

Evey, R. J. (1963), "The Theory and Application of Pushdown Store Machines," *Mathematical Linguistics and Automatic Translation*, Rep. no. NSF-10, Harvard Comput. Lab., Cambridge (Mass.).

Fillmore, C. J. (1966), "Toward a Modern Theory of Case," *The Ohio State University Res. Foundation Project on Ling. Analysis*, Rep. no. 13, pp. 1–24.

Firbas, J. (1961), "On the Communicative Value of the Modern English Finite Verb," *Brno Studies in English*, Vol. 3, pp. 79–104.

——— (1962), "Notes on the Function of the Sentence in the Act of Communication," *Sborník prací filosofické fakulty brněnské university* (*Miscellany of the Works of the Philos. Faculty of Brno University*), Vol. 11 A, no. 10, pp. 133–148.

——— (1964), "On Defining the Theme in Functional Sentence Analysis," *Travaux linguistiques de Prague*, Vol. 1, pp. 267–280.

Fitialov, S. J. (1961), "O postrojenii formal'noj morfologii v svjazi s mashinnym perevodom," *Doklady na konfer. po obrabotke informacii, mashin. perevodu i avtomat. chteniju teksta*, Vol. 2, Moscow.

Gaifman, C. (1961), "Dependency Systems and Phrase Structure Systems," P-2315, The RAND Corporation, Santa Monica.

Garvin, P. L. (1964), "On Linguistic Method," The Hague.

Godel, R. (1966), "F. de Saussure's Theory of Language," *Current Trends in Linguistics*, Vol. 3. (T. A. Sebeok, ed.), The Hague, pp. 479–493.

Goralčíková, A. and L. Nebeský (1968), "On a Possible Application of Pushdown-Store Transducers," *Prague Bulletin of Mathematical Linguistics*, 9, 10.

Halle, M. (1959), "The Sound Pattern of Russian," The Hague.

Halliday, M. A. K. (1967), "Notes on Transitivity and Theme in English," *Journ. of Linguistics*, 3, 37–81, 199ff.

Harper, K. E., and D. G. Hays (1960), "The Use of Machines in the Construction of a Grammar and Computer Program for Structural Analysis," *Information Processing*, Proc. of the Intern. Conference on Information Processing, Paris.

Hausenblas, K. (1958), "Syntaktická závislost, způsoby a prostředky jejího vyjadřování" (Syntactic Dependency, the Modes and Means of Expressing It), *Bulletin VŠRJL* (*Bulletin of the Institute of Russian Language and Literature*), Vol. 2, pp. 23–51.

Havelková, B. (1968), "Slovesná modalita v generativním popisu češtiny" (Verbal Modality in the Generative Description of Czech), *Acta Universitatis Carolinae, Slavica Pragensia*, Vol. 10, Prague.

Havránek, B. (1928, 1937), "Genera verbi v slovanských jazycích" (Verbal Voice in Slavonic Languages), Vol. 1, 2, Prague.

——— (1940), "Strukturální lingvistika" (Structural Linguistics), *Ottův slovník naučný nové doby* (*Otto's Encyclopaedia of Modern Times*), Vol. 6/1, Prague.

———, and A. Jedlička (1963), "Česká mluvnice" (Czech Grammar), Prague.

Hays, D. G. (1961), "Grouping and Dependency Theories," *Proc. of the National Symposium on MT* (H. P. Edmundson, ed.), Englewood Cliffs, pp. 258–266.

——— (1964), "Dependency Theory: A Formalism and Some Observations," *Language*, Vol. 40, pp. 511–525.

Hockett, C. F. (1961), "Linguistic Elements and Their Relations," *Language*, Vol. 37, pp. 29–53.

——— (1966), "Language, Mathematics, and Linguistics," *Current Trends in Ling.*, Vol. 3 (T. A. Sebeok, ed.), The Hague, pp. 155–304.

Hořejší, V. (1961), "Les plans linguistiques et la structure de l'énoncé," *Philologica Pragensia*, Vol. 4, pp. 193–203.

Householder, F. W. (1962), "On the Uniqueness of Semantic Mapping," *Word*, 18, pp. 173–185.

Ivanov, V. V. (1961), "K issledovaniju otnoshenij mezhdu kodami raznykh rangov," *Lingvisticheskije issledovanija po mashinnomu perevodu*, Vol. 2, Moscow, pp. 29–39.

Jakobson, R. (1936), "Beitrag zur allgemeinen Kasuslehre," *Travaux du Cercle linguistique de Prague*, Vol. 6, pp. 240–288.

———, C. G. M. Fant, and M. Halle (1952), "Preliminaries to Speech Analysis," Tech. Rep. No. 13, M. I. T. Acoustics Laboratory, Cambridge (Mass.).

———, and M. Halle (1956), "Fundamentals of Language," The Hague.

Jelínek, J. (1965), "A Linguistic Aspect of Transformation Rules", *Acta Universitatis Carolinae, Slavica Pragensia*, Vol. 7, Prague, pp. 81–86.

——— (1966), "Construct Classes," *Prague Studies in Mathematical Linguistics*, Vol. 1, pp. 167–182.

Karcevskij, S. (1929), "Du dualisme asymétrique du signe linguistique," *Travaux du Cercle linguistique de Prague*, Vol. 1, pp. 88–93; reprinted in Vachek (1964b).

Katz, J. J. (1964), "Mentalism in Linguistics," *Language*, Vol. 40, pp. 124–137.

——— (1966a), "The Semantic Component of a Linguistic Description," *Zeichen und System der Sprache*, Vol. 3, Berlin, pp. 195–224.

——— (1966b), "The Philosophy of Language," New York–London.

——— (1967), "Recent Issues in Semantic Theory," *Foundations of Language*, 3, pp. 124–194.

———, and P. M. Postal (1964), "An Integrated Theory of Linguistic Descriptions," Cambridge (Mass.).

Komrsková, S. (1968), "Příslovečné určení příčiny v generativním popisu češtiny" (The Adverbial of Cause in the Generative Description of Czech), Dissertation, Charles Univ., Prague.

Konečná, D. (1966), "K otázce druhů objektu podle významu" (On the Question of the Semantic Types of Objects), *Acta Universitatis Carolinae, Slavica Pragensia*, Vol. 8, pp. 311–316.

Kopečný, F. (1962) "Základy české skladby" (The Fundamentals of Czech Syntax), 2nd ed., Prague.

Kuryłowicz, J. (1935), "Études indoeuropéennes," Cracow.

——— (1936), "Dérivation lexicale et dérivation syntaxique," *Bulletin de la Société linguistique de Paris*, Vol. 37, pp. 79–92 (reprinted in Kuryłowicz, 1960).

——— (1948), "Les structures fondamentales de la langue: groupe et proposition," *Studia philosophica*, Vol. 3, pp. 203–209 (reprinted in Kuryłowicz, 1960).

——— (1956), "L'apophonie en indo-européen," Wrocław.

——— (1960), "Esquisses linguistiques," Wrocław.

——— (1964), "The Inflectional Categories of Indo-European," Heidelberg.

Lakoff, G., and J. R. Ross (1967), "Is Deep Structure Necessary?" Internal Memorandum, mimeographed.

Lamb, S. M. (1964a), "The Sememic Approach to Semantics," *American Anthropologist*, Vol. 66, no. 3, Part 2, pp. 57–78.

——— (1964b), "On Alternation, Transformation, Realization and Stratification," *Monograph Series on Languages and Linguistics*, no. 17, Report of the 15th Annual Round Table Meeting (C. I. J. M. Stuart, ed.), pp. 105–122.

——— (1966a), "Prolegomena to a Theory of Phonology," *Language*, Vol. 42, pp. 536–573.

——— (1966b), "Outline of Stratificational Grammar," Washington.

——— (1966c), "Epilegomena to a Theory of Language," *Romance Philology*, Vol. 19, pp. 531–573.

Lecerf, Y. (1960), "Programme des conflits, modèle des conflits," *La traduction automatique*, Vol. 1, no. 4, pp. 11–20; no. 5, pp. 17–36.

Marcus, S. (1963), "Linguistică matematică," Bucharest.

——— (1965), "Sur la notion de projectivité," *Zeitschrift für mathem. Logik und Grundl. d. Mathem.*, Vol. 11, pp. 181–192.

Mathesius, V. (1924), "Několik poznámek o funkci podmětu v moderní angličtině" (Some Remarks on the Function of Subject in Modern English), *Časopis pro moderní filologii*, Vol. 10, pp. 244–248.

——— (1929), "Zur Satzperspektive im modernen English," *Archiv für d. Studium d. neueren Sprachen u. Literaturen*, Vol. 155, pp. 202–210.

—— (1936), "On Some Problems of the Systematic Analysis of Grammar," *Travaux du Cercle linguistique de Prague*, 6, pp. 95–107; reprinted in Vachek (1964b).

——— (1961), "Obsahový rozbor současné angličtiny na základě obecně lingvistickém (A Functional Analysis of Present Day English on a General Linguistic Basis), Prague.

Mel'čuk, I. A. (1967), "Porozhdajushchaja grammatika—ili model', smysl-tekst'?," *Tezisy dokladov mezhvuz. konferencii po porozhd. grammatikam*, Tartu, pp. 67–69.

Morris, Ch. (1946), "Signs, Language and Behavior," New York.

Nebeský, L., and P. Sgall (1962), "Vztah formy a funkce v jazyce" (The Relation of Form and Function in Language), *Slovo a slovesnost*, Vol. 23, pp. 174–189; cf. the English Summary, *The Prague Bulletin of Mathematical Linguistics*, Vol. 1, 1964, pp. 29–37.

———, and P. Sgall (1965), "Relace a operace v syntaxi" (Relations and Operations in Syntax), *Slovo a slovesnost*, Vol. 26, pp. 218–223.

Novák, P. (1966a), "On the Three-Level Approach to Syntax", *Travaux linguistiques de Prague*, Vol. 2, pp. 219–223.

——— (1966b), "Závislostní koncepce v syntaxi" (The Dependency Conception in Syntax), Thesis, Charles University, Prague.

———, and P. Sgall (1962), "K otázce zákonů jazykového vývoje" (On the Question of the Laws of Language Development), *Acta Universitatis Carolinae*, *Philologica* 3, *Slavica Pragensia* 4, pp. 27–34.

——— and P. Sgall (1968), "On the Prague Functional Approach," *Travaux linguistiques de Prague*, Vol. 3.

Oettinger, A. G. (1961), "Automatic Syntactic Analysis and the Pushdown Store," *Structure of Language and Its Mathematical Aspects* (R. Jakobson, ed.), Proc. of the Symp. in Appl. Mathem., Vol. 12, pp. 104–129.

Palek, B. (1967), "Odkazování jako prostředek nadvětné syntaxe" (Cross-reference as a Means of Hypersyntax), Dissertation, Charles University, Prague.

——— (1968), "Cross-Reference: A Contribution to Hypersyntax," *Travaux linguistiques de Prague*, Vol. 3.

Panevová, J. (1967), "K voprosu o grammaticheskoj sinonimii v generativnom opisanii jazyka," *Prague Studies in Mathematical Linguistics*, Vol. 2, pp. 227–244.

——— (in prep.), "Závislá predikace v generativním popisu češtiny" (Dependent Predication in the Generative Description of Czech).

Pashchenko, N. (1965a), "Sintaksicheskij analiz i sopostavlenije sintaksicheskikh struktur cheshskogo i russkogo jazykov," Moscow.

——— (1965b), "Analiz i sopostavlenije sposobov vyrazhenija obstojatel'stvennykh vremennykh znachenij v russkom i cheshskom jazykakh," (*The Prague Bulletin of Mathematical Linguistics*, Vol. 3, pp. 13–37; Vol. 4, pp. 26–61.

Pauliny, E. (1943), "Štruktúra slovenského slovesa" (The Structure of the Slovak Verb), Bratislava.

Peirce, C. S. (1940), "The Philosophy of C. S. Peirce" (J. Buchler, ed.), New York.

Piťha, P. (1966), "On the Problem of Coordinate Conjunctions in the Analysis of Czech," *Prague Studies in Mathematical Linguistics*, Vol. 1, pp. 195–217.

——— (in press), "The Adverbial of Place in the Generative Description of Czech," *Prague Studies in Mathematical Linguistics*, Vol. 3.

———, and P. Sgall (in prep.), "Coordination in a Generative Description" (to appear in The Prague Bulletin of Mathem. Linguistics).

Pospíšil, D. (1966), "On a Linearization of Projective W-Trees," *The Prague Bulletin of Mathematical Linguistics*, Vol. 6, pp. 44–68.

Postal, P. M. (1964), "Constituent Structures," The Hague.

Putnam, H. (1961), "Some Issues in the Theory of Grammar," *Structure of Language and Its Mathem. Aspects* (R. Jakobson, ed.), Proc. of Symp. in Appl. Mathem., Vol. 12, pp. 25–42.

Quine, W. V. (1960), "Word and Object," Cambridge (Mass.)—New York—London.

Revzin, I. I. (1957), "Struktural'naja lingvistika i problemy izuchenija slova," *Voprosy jazykoznanija*, Vol. 6, no. 2, pp. 31–41.

——— (1961), "Formal'nyj i semanticheskij analiz sintaksicheskikh svjazej v jazyke," *Primenenija logiki v nauke i tekhnike*, Moscow, pp. 119–139.

———, and V. J. Rozencvejg (1964), "Osnovy obshchego i mashinnogo perevoda", Moscow.
Saussure, F. de (1916), "Cours de linguistique générale"; quoted here from the English translation by W. Baskin, "Course in General Linguistics," New York, 1959.
Schnelle, H. (1963), "Programmieren linguistischer Automaten," *Neuere Ergebnisse der Kybernetik* (K. Steinbach and S. W. Wagner, eds.), Munich, pp. 109–136.
Sgall, P. (1960), "Soustava pádových koncovek v češtině" (The System of Czech Case Endings), *Acta Universitatis Carolinae, Slavica Pragensia*, Vol. 2, pp. 65–84.
——— (1963), "Odpověď na otázku č. III.25." (Reply to Question no. 3.25), *Slavjanskaja filologija*, Vol. 1, Sofia, pp. 238f.
——— (1964), "Zur Frage der Ebenen im Sprachsystem," *Travaux linguistiques de Prague*, Vol. 1, pp. 95–106.
——— (1966), "Ein mehrstufiges generatives System," *Kybernetika*, Vol. 2, pp. 181–190.
——— (1967a), "Generativní popis jazyka a česká deklinace" (A Generative Description of Language and the Czech Declension), Prague.
——— (1967b), "Zur Eingliederung der Semantik in die Sprachbeschreibung," *Folia Linguistica*, Vol. 1, pp. 18–22.
——— (1967c), "Functional Sentence Perspective in a Generative Description," *Prague Studies in Mathematical Linguistics*, Vol. 2, pp. 203–225.
——— (1968), "Porjadok slov i aktual'noje chlenenije predlozhenija v generativnom opisanii slavjanskikh jazykov," *Československé přednášky pro VI. mezin. sjezd slavistů* (*Czechoslovak Contributions to the Sixth Intern. Congress of Slavists*), Prague.
Skalička V. (1935), "Zur ungarischen Grammatik," Prague; cf. also an extract (pp. 12–20) in Vachek (1964b).
——— (1948), "Kodaňský strukturalismus a 'pražská škola'" (The Copenhagen Structuralism and the 'Prague School'), *Slovo a slovesnost*, Vol. 10, pp. 115–142.
——— (1962), "Das Wesen der Morphologie und der Syntax," *Acta Universitatis Carolinae, Slavica Pragensia*, Vol. 4, pp. 123–127
Staal, J. F. (1967), "Some Semantic Relations between Sentoids," *Foundations of Language*, Vol. 3, pp. 66–88.
Šmilauer, V. (1947), "Novočeská skladba" (Modern Czech Syntax), Prague (2nd ed. 1966).
——— (1957), "Učebnice větného rozboru" (Text-Book of Sentence Analysis), Prague.
Tesnière, L. (1959), "Éléments de syntaxe structurale," Paris.
Tiede, H. (1966), "Matematické postupy při budování generativních gramatik" (Mathematical Methods Used in Generative Grammars), Dissertation, Charles University, Prague.
Trnka, B. (1958), "Morfologické protiklady" (Morphological Oppositions), *O vědeckém poznání soudobých jazyků* (*On the Research into Contemporary Languages*), Prague, pp. 93–104.
——— (1961), "Principles of Morphological Analysis", *Philologica Pragensia*, Vol. 4, pp. 129–137.
——— (1964), "On the Linguistic Sign in the Multilevel Organization of Language," *Travaux Linguistiques de Prague*, Vol. 1, pp. 33–40.
Vachek, J. (1955), "Notes on the So-called Complex Condensation in Modern English," *Sborník prací filos. fak. brněnské university*, A 3, 63–77.
——— (1961), "Some Less Familiar Aspects of the Analytical Trend of English," *Brno Studies in English* 3, Prague, pp. 9ff.
——— (1964a), "On Some Basic Principles of 'Classical' Phonology," *Zeitschrift für Phonetik, Sprachwissenschaft und Kommunikationsforschung*, Vol. 17, pp. 409–431.
——— (1964b), "A Prague School Reader in Linguistics," Bloomington.
——— (in press), " Základy české fonologie a morfonologie" (Outline of the Phonology and Morphonology of Czech), Prague.
Weinreich, U. (1966), "Explorations in Semantic Theory," *Current Trends in Linguistics*, Vol. 3 (T. A. Sebeok, ed.), The Hague, pp. 395–478.
Zawadowski, L. (1967), "Le Temps Linguistique," *Kwartalnik neofilologiczny* 14, 415–429.
Zimmermann, Ilse (1967), "Die Funktionen der Nominalphrasen im Satz" (submitted at the 1967 Conference on Transformational Grammar, Berlin), mimeographed.

INDEX

In the case of authors listed herein, numbers set in *italics* designate the page numbers on which the complete literature citation is given.